Qur'anic the Greatest Divine Name

Verses Containing the Greatest Name of Allāh سبحانه وتعالى

WITH ORIGINAL ARABIC TEXT,
ENGLISH TRANSLATION,
TRANSLITERATION,
COMPILATION & EXPLANATION

SHAYKH MUHAMMAD HISHAM KABBANI

FOREWORD BY
SHAYKH MUHAMMAD NAZIM AL-HAQQANI

INSTITUTE FOR SPIRITUAL & CULTURAL ADVANCEMENT

First Edition January 2021

ISBN: 978-1-938058-59-2

Printed in the United States of America.

Library of Congress Cataloging-in-Publication Data

Names: Kabbani, Muhammad Hisham, author.

Title: Qur'anic openings to the greatest divine name : verses containing the greatest name of Allāh : with original Arabic text, English translation & transliteration compilation & explanation / Shaykh Muhammad Hisham Kabbani.

Other titles: Qur'an. Selections.

Description: Fenton : Institute for Spiritual and Cultural Understanding, 2021. | In English and Arabic.

Identifiers: LCCN 2020055220 | ISBN 9781938058592 (paperback)

Subjects: LCSH: God (Islam)--Qur'anic teaching. | God (Islam)--Worship and love.

Classification: LCC BP134.G6 K33 2021 | DDC 297.2/11--dc23

LC record available at https://lccn.loc.gov/2020055220

Published and Distributed by:

Institute for Spiritual and Cultural Advancement

17195 Silver Parkway, #401
Fenton, MI 48430 USA
Tel: (888) 278-6624
Fax:(810) 815-0518

Email: info@sufilive.com
Web: http://www.sufilive.com

أعوذ بالله من الشيطان الرجيم بسم الله الرحمن الرحيم

Sūratu 'l-Fātiḥa and the first verses of Sūratu 'l-Baqarah.

A'ūdhu billāhi min ash-shayṭāni 'r-rajīm.

Bismillāhi 'r-Raḥmāni 'r-Raḥīm.

Alif. Lām. Mīm.

This is the Book about which there is no doubt, a Guidance for those conscious of Allāh, who believe in the Unseen, establish prayer and spend out of what We have provided for them. And those who believe in what has been revealed to you, (O Muḥammad), and what was revealed before you and of the Hereafter, they are certain (in faith). Those are upon Guidance from their Lord, and it is those who are the successful!

(Sūratu 'l-Baqarah, 2:1-5)

Contents

Intention

Aʿūdhu billāhi min ash-shayṭāni 'r-rajīm.

Bismillāhi 'r-Raḥmāni 'r-Raḥīm.

نَوَيْتُ الأَرْبَعِين، نَوَيْتُ الإِعْتِكَاف نَوَيْتُ الخَلْوَة نَوَيْتُ العُزْلَة، نَوَيْتُ
الرِيَاضَة نَوَيْتُ السُّلُوك، لِلهِ تَعالىٰ فى هَذَا المَسْجِد

Nawaytu 'l-arbaʿīn, nawaytu 'l-ʿitikāf, nawaytu 'l-khalwa, nawaytu 'l-ʿuzla, nawaytu 'r-riyāḍa, nawaytu 's-sulūk, lillāhi taʿala fī hādhā 'l-masjid.

I intend the forty (days of seclusion); I intend seclusion in the mosque; I intend seclusion; I intend isolation; I intend discipline (of the ego); I intend to travel in God's Path for the sake of God in this mosque.

أَطِيعُواْ اللّهَ وَأَطِيعُواْ الرَّسُولَ وَأُوْلِي الأَمْرِ مِنكُمْ

Atiʿūllāha wa atiʿū 'r-Rasūla wa ūli 'l-amri minkum.

Obey Allāh, obey the Prophet, and obey those in authority among you.[1]

---

[1] Sūrat an-Nisā', 4:59.

اللَّهُمَّ صَلِّ عَلىٰ مُحَمَّدٍ حَتّىٰ يَرضَىٰ سَيِدِناَ مُحَمَّدٍ

Allāhumma salli 'alā Sayyīdinā Muḥammad ḥattā yarḍā Sayyīdinā Muḥammad.

O Allāh exalt our master Muḥammad until our master Muḥammad is well-pleased.

الله

Shaykh Muhammad Nazim al-Haqqani ق reading Holy Qur'an.

Foreword

The Book About Which There is No Doubt

A'ūdhu billāhi min ash-shayṭāni 'r-rajīm.

Bismillāhi 'r-Raḥmāni 'r-Raḥīm.

Allāh Almighty ﷻ begins the Holy Qur'an, after *al-Fātiḥa*, the Opening Chapter, by saying, *Bismillāhi 'r-Raḥmāni 'r-Raḥīm*:

الٓمٓ ذَٰلِكَ ٱلْكِتَٰبُ لَا رَيْبَ ۛ فِيهِ ۛ هُدًى لِّلْمُتَّقِينَ

Alif. Lām. Mīm. Dhālika 'l-kitābu lā rayba fīhi huda 'l-li 'l-muttaqīn.

Alif. Lām. Mīm. This is the Book about which there is no doubt, a Guidance for those conscious of Allāh.[2]

These three letters, "*Alif. Lām. Mīm.* (الم)," are only a cipher, a code between Allāh Almighty and His Prophet ﷺ. However, sometimes Allāh Almighty lets some of His Beloved Servants know the secrets of letters. Each letter carries endless secrets, and they are keys to the Holy Qur'an. The Holy Qur'an is endless oceans, not only one ocean!

When Allāh Almighty says, "*Alif* (ا)," the first letter of the Arabic alphabet, it signifies for us an endless ocean. And as often as He repeats "*Alif,*" each one of those *Alifs* signifies another endless ocean and you cannot find the same meanings in each *Alif*. Maybe in the Holy Qur'an you can find thousands and thousands of *Alifs*, each one representing an endless ocean of Divine Knowledge. We may know something according to our capacity.

---

[2] Sūratu 'l-Baqarah, 2:1-2.

As *Sulṭān al-Mufassirīn*, the king of those who have explained the Holy Qur'an, Ibn 'Abbās ⁂ (the son of the Prophet's uncle) said, "The letter *Alif* signifies the Name of Allāh Almighty, *Lām* signifies the angel Gabriel ⁂, and *Mīm* signifies Prophet Muḥammad ⁂."

O People! Without doubt, that Holy Book has come from Allāh Almighty, from His Divine Presence to Prophet Muḥammad ⁂ through the angel Gabriel. No one can have any doubt that Book is from Allāh Almighty! Allāh ⁂ says, "*Lā rayba fīh, no doubt in it*," so that it takes away all doubts from everyone, because Man is full of doubts and if he wants to fill every doubt by himself, he cannot do it without using that Holy Book. Yes, it covers all doubts! For all people, no matter how many different doubts there may be, they are going to be filled by the Holy Qur'an, the Glorious Qur'an. They are going to be like the holes of ants: when a river floods a place, which holes can remain? It fills them and goes on.

Therefore, first came the prophets, and we have been ordered to believe in the prophets so that it is possible for us to believe in God Almighty. If you do not give your trust to an individual person, you cannot have belief in God Almighty. Therefore, Allāh Almighty says that "You must believe in My Prophet, My Beloved Muḥammad ⁂, that he has been given a Book from his Lord Almighty through Gabriel ⁂, *dhālika 'l-kitāb*.

Without any doubt, you must believe that he ﷺ has brought you that Holy Book, the Glorious Qur'an, from My Divine Presence through Gabriel, and you have to trust in his individual existence as a prophet. Then, everything is going to be all right; otherwise, it is impossible!"

Dive into Holy Verse Oceans

May Allāh Almighty give us from His Divine Wisdom, because we may have knowledge, but if no wisdom, knowledge is going to do nothing. We are in need of wisdom, and a little wisdom is more important than all of this world's knowledge. Knowledge cannot push or pull you, but wisdom may pull you or push you. In wisdom there is power. Therefore, knowledge without wisdom never gives benefit.

If knowledge could give benefit to anyone, it would have given it to Satan, as he was the first in knowledge, knowing the Gospel, the Torah, the Psalms, and the Holy Qur'an. No one among scholars can compete with him, as he comes first. He knows so much, but without wisdom; he had so much knowledge without wisdom, and then he fell! Therefore, it is not important to learn so much or to know so much, but it is important to ask for some wisdom from Allāh Almighty. Even one wisdom is going to be enough for you forever, to take you to happiness and peace here and Hereafter, to our Lord's Pleasure.

Allāh Almighty sent 6,666 verses in the Holy Qur'an. Each verse is like an endless ocean, and the oceans are full of precious pearls, but if pearls could be had easily, they would be cheap. Why are pearls precious, valuable? Because pearls can be found in the deepest places in the seas, and the dangerous places, also. Allāh Almighty always makes something valuable precious, protected, so that it is not easily reached. You cannot have a rose without thorns and a treasure without dragons! Everything you can get easily is cheap. You can buy tomatoes, potatoes and onions anywhere, but rubies, diamonds, pearls, you cannot find everywhere, although you can find so many made of glass.

Therefore, from oceans you may take fishes or shells; the sea throws shells on the beach, but it never throws pearls. Every verse of the Holy Qur'an is like endless oceans; the one who makes himself dive in may take. How would a person dive into the sea with clothes? No one dives into the deep-sea wearing clothes; they like to take off as much as they can for diving. For Verse Oceans, for the Oceans of the Holy Qur'an, you must take off everything and then you may dive into them!

What are you going to take off? Not things like these clothes, but you must take off from your heart everything belonging to this world; you must take away *dunyā* from your heart, this world's pleasures, and you must know what *dunyā* is. Everything that engages or occupies you from your Lord and you have enjoyment from is *dunyā*; everything that occupies a servant from his Lord is *dunyā*!

This is the most important point for everyone, for every Believer, whether his faith may be Jewish, Christian or Muslim: when Allāh Almighty looks at their hearts, by whom are their hearts occupied? Is that heart engaged by Himself alone, or by *dunyā*?

You must know that Allāh Almighty gives permission for all of your body that it may work, may be engaged by this life, except for your heart. You may be occupied in your body, it doesn't matter, because we live in this life and we have some responsibilities. Allāh Almighty gives permission for our organs to go, to come, to look, to do, but He says, "Only your heart: don't let it be engaged in *dunyā*."

Keep your heart for your Lord alone and He is going to be pleased with you. When He is pleased with you, He is going to make you pleased with Him! That is *as-Sa'ādat al-Kubrā*, the Greatest Happiness; you will have been given endless happiness when Allāh Almighty makes you pleased. We are asking His pleasure with us. We are trying to make him pleased with us. Everything except that does not give our Lord pleasure with us. Complete pleasure from Allāh Almighty with His Servants is when His Servants give their hearts to Him Almighty!

Shaykh Muhammad Nazim al-Haqqani an-Naqshbandi
Summer 1984/Ramadan 1404
London, UK

الله

Shaykh Hisham Kabbani with his son Dr. Nour Kabbani, ق reading the Holy Qur'an.

Preface

A Guidance for Those Who Believe in the Unseen

أعُوذُ بِاللهِ من الشَّيْطانِ الرَّجيم.

بِسْمِ اللهِ الرَّحْمٰنِ الرَّحِيمِ

Aʿūdhu billāhi min ash-shayṭāni 'r-rajīm

Bismillāhi 'r-Raḥmāni 'r-Raḥīm.

May Allāh ﷻ bless the soul of Grandshaykh Mawlānā Shaykh Nazim, raise his stations higher and higher, and may his gaze always be upon us. He says things that are from the *Ghayb*, Unseen; what he talks about is something that is unseen to us, and in the Holy Qur'an, we are asked to believe in the Unseen:

ٱلَّذِينَ يُؤْمِنُونَ بِٱلْغَيْبِ

Alladhīna yu'minūna bi 'l-ghayb.

(Those) who believe in the Unseen.[3]

Allāh ﷻ is saying, "This Qur'an is *Hudā*, Guidance to the ones who believe in the *Ghayb*, Unseen, so prepare yourselves to hear from the Unseen!"

When we open the Holy Qur'an, most of it is from the Unseen. Sometimes Allāh ﷻ talks about the prophets, such as Sayyīdinā Mūsā عليه السلام and Sayyīdinā Ibrāhīm ﷺ. These were historical facts that were seen, but when Allāh ﷻ tells what's prepared for us in the Hereafter, it is Unseen. Therefore, a Muslim, a *Mu'min* has to prepare himself or herself to accept the Unseen, the Unknown.

Mawlānā Shaykh Nazim ق says that when you open the Holy Qur'an, the minimum amount of meanings that appear to the saints from every

---

[3] Sūratu 'l-Baqarah, 2:3.

letter is 24,000, because the saint looks with the Light of Allāh ﷻ and the Light of Sainthood. We only see a drawing, a line, or hear a sound or pronunciation, but when the saint uses the power Allāh ﷻ has given to him, he can extract 24,000 meanings, and that is at the lowest level!

Mawlānā Shaykh Nazim ق says that each letter from the Arabic alphabet is an ocean, beginning from the letter *Alif* (ا), which is pronounced as "*ā*". In English, you say the letter A, but in Arabic you don't say A, you say the name of that letter, which is *Alif* (ا) spelled out in three letters: *Alif, Lām, Fā* (ا ل ف). And the first letter of *Alif* (ا ل ف) is another *Alif* (ا), so you get another three letters! So now you are down to one, three and another three from one. The more you break down that letter, the more letters you get!

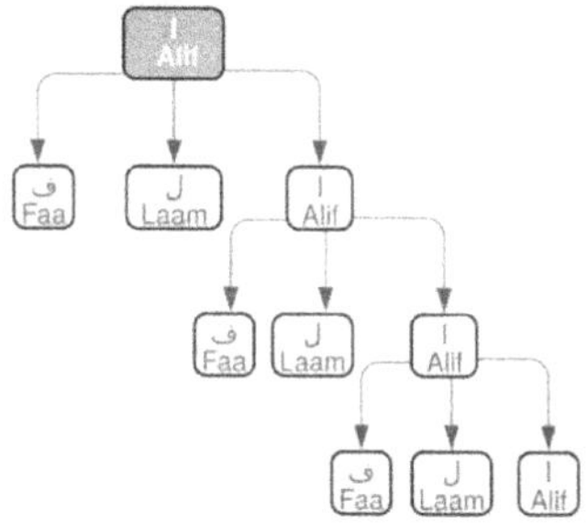

So, when you separate each letter of Holy Qur'an, you get more and more letters under it, and each time you separate another one of these letters, you get more and more! For example, Mawlānā gives the example in Sūrat Maryam, where Allāh ﷻ

says, "*Kāf* (ك). *Hā* (ه). Yā (ى). 'Ayn (ع). Sād. (ص)." The letter *Kāf* is three letters: *Kāf* (ك), *Alif* (ا), *Fā* (ف). Under the *Kāf* is another three letters (كاف); under the *Alif*, another three letters (الف); and under the *Fā*, another three letters (فاء). So, from one letter you went down to nine letters, and if you keep breaking it down, you will keep getting more and more letters. It's an ocean!

From just one letter, from one *Alif*, the knowledge that can come out is at least 24,000 meanings. What the Prophet ﷺ has known from the meanings of that one *Alif* no one else can know, not even the pronunciation, as the Prophet ﷺ comes with both the words and the pronunciations!

SubḥānAllāh, *Alif* is a designation for *adh-Dhāt*, the Essence of Allāh ﷻ. *Alif* (ا) is the first letter of "Allāh (الله)," so that Divine Presence is hidden in each letter of the Arabic alphabet.

Take any letter, for example: *Bā* (باء) has an *Alif* in the middle; *Tā* (تاء) has an *Alif* in the middle; *Thā* (ثاء) has an *Alif* in the middle. Where is the *Alif* in *Jīm* (جيم)? In the *Yā* (ياء), as the letter *Jīm* is: *Jīm* (ج), *Yā* (ى), *Mīm* (م), and *Yā* has an *Alif* in the middle. *Hā* (حاء) has an *Alif* in the middle; *Qāf* (قاف) has an *Alif*. Where is the *Alif* in the *Nūn* (نون)? In the *wāw* (واو)! So, in *Nūn*, *Alif* is hidden in the letter *Wāw* (و). So that letter which represents the Divine Presence, *Alif*, is in each letter of the Arabic alphabet! That hidden *Alif* in each letter of the Arabic alphabet represents the Divine Presence, and there is no limit to what is in the Divine Presence.

That's why, each Arabic letter is an ocean of knowledge, because it's related directly or indirectly to the Divine Presence, and there is no limit to what's in the Divine Presence. And what the Prophet ﷺ has from the meanings of that one letter is the highest of all saints and prophets, as no one can reach his knowledge.

So, imagine, you open the Holy Qur'an and you read one word: you can dive in that one word and disappear! If you are a saint, you would go into that one word and with each time you dissect the letter into the three letters it represents, each time you go further and deeper, as there is no limit; you keep diving in, and you find yourself in the Divine Presence, extracting meanings!

SubḥānAllāh, look at the power of Allāh ﷻ! Even the simplest things, like the writing, the letters, how Allāh ﷻ puts secrets and power in them, because they are coming from Him. Everything that Allāh ﷻ creates also has limitless power, because it's coming from Allāh's creations, from these oceans.

So, when that holy verse, *"Kāf. Hā. Yā. ʿAyn. Ṣād."* came down with Sayyīdinā Jibrīl ؑ to the Prophet ﷺ, the Prophet ﷺ said, "I knew it!" As

Grandshaykh is quoting, Sayyīdinā Jibrīl ﷺ said, "*Yā Rasūlullāh* ﷺ! This is the first time I'm coming to you with this verse. How did you know before I knew?" And Grandshaykh ق said, "That is an evidence that the Prophet ﷺ has a direct connection with the Divine Presence, without any intermediary, and the evidence is in the Holy Qur'an, where Allāh ﷻ says:

Asta'īdhu bi 'Llāh:

وَإِنَّكَ لَتُلَقَّى الْقُرْآنَ مِن لَّدُنْ حَكِيمٍ عَلِيمٍ

As for you, (O Muḥammad), the Qur'an is bestowed upon you from the Presence of One Who is Wise and All-Knowing.[4]

Allāh ﷻ is confirming that *Rasūlullāh* ﷺ receives directly from the Divine Presence: *Wa innaka*, verily and surely, *la tulaqqā*, there is no doubt about it that you are receiving with power, with might! "*Talaqqī*" means, "You are receiving something with power." "*Laqa*" means to take or to receive (something), but when you say "*Laqqa*," with a *shadda* (double pronunciation of the letter *Qāf*), that means it is coming with power. Allāh ﷻ is saying, "You are receiving the Qur'an with power straight from the Presence of an All-Wise, All-Knower. "*Min ladun*," means from the Presence, from That One, without any

---

[4] Sūratu 'n-Naml, 27:6.

intermediary! "You are receiving directly from the Presence of That One Who is All-Wise and All-Knowing."

However, Grandshaykh ق is saying, "*Wa lākin adaban,* but to keep with *adab*, manners, as *Rasūlullāh* has the highest manners, *Rasūlullāh* ﷺ was accepting to take the revelation from Sayyīdinā Jibrīl عليه السلام and was receiving it." But truly, in *ḥaqīqah,* in reality, he had no barrier, no veil, nothing between him and the Divine Presence!

That means, *Rasūlullāh* ﷺ has reached such a high level and has gone beyond any level that any prophet has reached. Prophets received revelation through Sayyīdinā Jibrīl عليه السلام, but Sayyīdinā *Rasūlullāh* ﷺ receives revelation without the means of Sayyīdinā Jibrīl عليه السلام. That means he has reached such a perfection that he is in the Divine Presence without any veil between him and the Divine Presence: "Surely, you are receiving from the Presence of That One." And actually, *Rasūlullāh* is the veil between the Divine Presence and us! He has no veil between him and the Lord, but *Rasūlullāh* ﷺ is the one that protects us from being burned and consumed.

So, what he is receiving from Sayyīdinā Jibrīl عليه السلام is the pronunciation and the words, as Grandshaykh ق is saying, but *Rasūlullāh* ﷺ is receiving directly from Allāh ﷻ the realities of Holy Qur'an. So, with Sayyīdinā Jibrīl عليه السلام comes the words and pronunciation, but from the Divine Presence comes the realities of the Holy Qur'an.

Sayyīdinā Muḥammad ﷺ is the Prophet and the Messenger of Realities, and he is receiving the Realities of Holy Qur'an directly from the Divine Presence!

Dr. Nour Mohamad Kabbani
24 June 2017/29 Ramadan 1438
Fenton Zawiya, Michigan

الله

About the Author

A descendant of the Prophet Muḥammad ﷺ, Shaykh Muhammad Hisham Kabbani, is a world-renowned religious scholar and author, who hails from a long line of illustrious traditional Islamic scholars, including the former head of the Association of Muslim Scholars of Lebanon and the present Grand Mufti of Lebanon.

Shaykh Kabbani is highly trained, both as a Western scientist and as a classical Islamic scholar. He has devoted his life to the promotion of the traditional Islamic principles of peace, tolerance, love and compassion, while exposing extremism in all its forms.

He received a bachelor's degree in chemistry and studied medicine. He also holds a degree in Islamic Divine Law, and under the tutelage of Shaykh 'AbdAllāh Daghestani ق, license to teach, guide and counsel religious students in Islamic spirituality from Shaykh Muhammad Nazim Adil al-Qubrusi al-Haqqani an-Naqshbandi ق, the world leader of the Naqshbandi-Haqqani Sufi Order.

Shaykh Kabbani has spent numerous years teaching hidden wisdoms of the Holy Qur'an to his students worldwide, including an extensive series of commentary on various chapters of the Qur'an. As a prophetic inheritor, his character has been described as that of a walking Qur'an.

From childhood, he was known to have a beautiful, melodious recitation of the Qur'an and was often called "The Little Abdul Basit," after an Egyptian Qur'an reciter who gained the reputation of being called "The Voice of Heaven" due to his melodious style, remarkable breath control, and unique emotional and engaging tone, which Shaykh Kabbani also received as a God-given gift.

Shaykh Kabbani contributes to the world a vast background in Islamic Law and Tradition, but delivers his message humbly and clearly, which immediately strikes a chord with a wide global audience. It is his rare combination of humility and authority that makes his influence so wide-reaching.

In the U.S., Shaykh Kabbani serves as Chairman, Islamic Supreme Council of America; Founder, Naqshbandi Sufi Order of America; Advisor, World Organization for Resource Development and Education; Chairman, Kamilat Muslim Women's Organization; and, Founder and President, The Muslim Magazine.

He books include: *Call On Me* (2019); *Hierarchy of Saints* (2016); *The Fiqh of Islam* (2014); *Ṣalawāt of Tremendous Blessings* (2012); *The Peacemakers* (2012); *Jihad: Principles of Leadership in War and Peace* (2010); *Banquet for the Soul* (2008); *A Spiritual Commentary on the Chapter of Sincerity* (2006); *Sufi Science of Self Realization* (Fons Vitae, 2005); *Keys to the Divine Kingdom* (2005); *Classical Islam and the Naqshbandi Sufi Order* (2004); *The Naqshbandi Sufi Tradition Guidebook* (2004); *The Approach of*

Armageddon? An Islamic Perspective (2003); *Encyclopedia of Prophet Muḥammad's Women Companions and the Traditions They Related* (1998, with Dr. Laleh Bakhtiar); *Encyclopedia of Islamic Doctrine* (7 vols. 1998); *Angels Unveiled* (1996); *The Naqshbandi Sufi Way* (1995); *Remembrance of God Liturgy of the Sufi Naqshbandi Masters* (1994).

الله

Publisher's Notes

References from the Qur'an and the *ḥadīth* (holy traditions) are most commonly italicized and offset. References from the Qur'an are noted in parenthesis, i.e. (3:127), indicating the third chapter, verse 127. References from *ḥadīth* are attributed to their transmitter, i.e. Bukhārī, Muslim, Ahmed, etc. Quotes from other sources are offset without italics.

Dates of events are characterized as "AH/CE," which infers "after Hijrah (migration)" on which the Islamic calendar is based, and "Christian Era," respectively.

Muslims around the world typically offer praise upon speaking, hearing, or reading the name "Allāh" and any of the Islamic names of God. Muslims also offer salutation and/or invoke blessing upon speaking, hearing or reading the names of Prophet Muḥammad, other prophets, his family, his companions, and saints. We have applied the following international standards, using Arabic calligraphy and lettering:

﷾ *subḥānahu wa taʿalā* (Glorified and Exalted), after the proper name of God, "*Allāh*" in Arabic.

ﷺ *ṣall-Allāhu ʿalayhi wa sallam* (God's blessings and greetings of peace be upon him) following the names of the Prophet.

عليه السلام *ʿalayhi 's-salām* (peace be upon him) following the names of other prophets, angels, and Khiḍr.

عليها السلام *ʿalayhā 's-salām* (peace be upon her) following the name Mary, the mother of Jesus, peace be upon them both.

رضي الله عنه/رضي الله عنها *radī-Allāhu ʿanhu/ʿanhā* (may God be pleased with him/her) following the name of a male or female companion of the Prophet ﷺ.

ق *qaddas-Allāhu sirrah* (may God sanctify his secret) following the name of a saint.

Transliteration

Transliteration is provided in the glossaries and in the section on the spiritual practices to facilitate correct pronunciation and is based on the following system:

Symbol	Transliteration	Symbol	Transliteration	Vowels:	
ء	ʼ	ط	ṭ	Long	
ب	b	ظ	ẓ	آ ى	ā
ت	t	ع	ʻ	و	ū
ث	th	غ	gh	ى	ī
ج	j	ف	f	Short	
ح	ḥ	ق	q	ـَ	a
خ	kh	ك	k	ـُ	u
د	d	ل	l	ـِ	i
ذ	dh	م	m		
ر	r	ن	n		
ز	z	ه	h		
س	s	و	w		
ش	sh	ى	y		
ص	ṣ	ة	ah; at		
ض	ḍ	ال	al-/'l-		

الله

Introduction

Celebrate the Noble Qur’an and Love of the Noble Prophet ﷺ

A‘ūdhu billāhi min ash-shayṭāni 'r-rajīm.

Bismillāhi 'r-Raḥmāni 'r-Raḥīm.

Greetings of Peace, Mercy and the Blessings of Allāh ﷻ be upon you, O Lovers and Beloved Ones of the Prophet of Allāh ﷺ! O Lovers and Beloved Ones of the Companions, the scholars, the reciters of the Holy Qur’an, the Righteous Saints, and the scholars and reciters of the Holy Qur'an who practice what they know, the reading and recitation of the Holy Qur'an!

Alḥamdulillāh, glory, praise and thanks be to Allāh ﷻ, Who has made us part of the Nation of His Elect, the Prophet ﷺ, Sayyīdinā Muḥammad ﷺ, a nation that is truly beloved on the part of the Truth, Allāh ﷻ, a nation that is truly beloved on the part of the Prophet ﷺ, and a nation that is truly beloved from within the blessed chest of the Prophet ﷺ, and in his heart.

Glory, praise and thanks be to Allāh ﷻ! We glorify Him and we seek His Help and His Guidance. We seek refuge in Allāh ﷻ from the evil of our own selves and from the evil of our deeds. Whoever

Allāh ﷻ guides, there is no one to lead astray and whoever He leads astray, there is no one that can guide him aright.

We have spoken much in the past and every moment elapsing is in the past, because time is passing quickly for the Nation and is spent quickly in the teaching of the Holy Qur'an. *Inshā-Allāh,* we love the Holy Qur'an and we have been guided through the guidance of the Holy Qur'an!

There are huge and momentous events taking place aimed at the stopping of the teaching of the Holy Qur'an, but the Prophet ﷺ is the carrier of Holy Qur'an by the virtue of the Power and Might of Allāh, Most High!

We are passing through a time that is rife with problems and obstacles, and we say:

إِنَّا لِلّهِ وَإِنَّـا إِلَيْهِ رَاجِعونَ

Innā lillāhi wa innā ilayhi rāji'ūn.

Unto Allāh we belong and to Him do we return.[5]

Whoever dies as a Muslim, then forgiveness of their sins is their lot and theirs is the love of the Prophet ﷺ.

[5] Sūratu 'l-Baqarah, 2:156.

The year 1442 has arrived and we are now in the era where the *Awlīyāullāh* obtained blessings from the era of the Prophet ﷺ; the Great Message of the Holy Qur'an came to the Prophet ﷺ filled with news of love of the Friends of Allāh and love of the Companions of the Prophet ﷺ. The Companions obtained blessings by means of the Prophet ﷺ, and we are hoping to obtain the blessings of the Prophet ﷺ.

The Prophet ﷺ is our heart! The Prophet ﷺ is our love! The Prophet ﷺ is our might and our honor, and the Prophet ﷺ loves his Nation!

Therefore, we must make ourselves tread the Path according to the sayings and *Aḥadīth* of the Prophet ﷺ. We ask and hope from Allāh Most High that He accept this from us and that He will cover us and our faults with His Beautiful Concealment. Glory, praise and thanks be to Allāh ﷻ, the Lord of the Worlds!

Twenty years ago, was a time they rejected celebrating the birth of the Prophet ﷺ and I faced forceful opposition to my efforts to renew its celebration after it had been suspended due to some people who were paid to prevent its remembrance in the US.

Glory, praise and thanks be to Allāh ﷻ, we have reached the brink of a pit and that brink is very short indeed, but despite that there is a huge strength in it.

So, take on the religion of the Prophet Muḥammad ﷺ! When the Prophet ﷺ ascended on the Night of *Miʿrāj*, the Companions and the *Awlīyā* were singing, and their recitation was a staggering miracle of beauty. They learned the well-known power that is known as *Mawlid an-Nabī* ﷺ, the Celebration of the Birth of the Prophet ﷺ!

There would be no mosque in existence if not for our Prophet ﷺ. He is our exemplar, our paradigm and our Beloved, and for him is our passionate longing! *Inshā-Allāh* we hope this festival of the New Islamic Year is a festival among the brethren and between the Prophet ﷺ and the *Muḥammadan Ummah.*

Many among the sayings and actions of the Prophet ﷺ are spreading far and wide at this time, and they are mentioned in the *nashīds*. Our duty is to hold fast to those *nashīds*, after the reading of the Holy Qur'an in our schools with our children and with love among our brethren.

After that, we recite "*Ṭalaʿa 'l-Badru ʿAlaynā*, The Full Moon Rose Over Us from the Valley of Wadaʿ" [reference to the entrance of the Prophet ﷺ into *Madīnatu 'l-Munawwara*]:

(١) طَلَعَ البَدْرُ عَلَينَا   مِنْ ثَنِيَاتِ الوَدَاعِ

Ṭalaʿa 'l-badru ʿalaynā, min thanīyāti 'l-wadāʿ.

O the Full Moon rose above us from the Valley of Wadaʿ.

(٢) وَجَبَ الشُكرُ عَلَينَا   مَا دَعَا للهِ دَاعِ

Wajaba *'sh-shukru ʿalaynā, mā daʿā li 'Llāhi dāʿ.*

Gratitude is our obligation as long as any caller calls to Allāh.

(٣) أَيُّهَا المَبْعُوثُ فِينَا   جِئتَ بِالأَمرِ المُطَاعِ

Ayyuha 'l-mabʿūthu fīnā, ji'ta bi 'l-amri 'l-mutāʿ.

O you who were sent among us! You came with the orders to be obeyed.

(٤) كُنْ شَفِيعًا يَا حَبِيبِى   يَومَ حَشرٍ وَاجْتِمَاعِ

Kun shafīʿan yā ḥabībī, yawma ḥashrin w' ajtimāʿ.

Be our intercessor, O our Beloved, on the Day of Collection and Gathering.

(٥) رَبَّنَا صَلِّ عَلَى مَنْ   حَلَّ فِى خَيرِ البِقَاعِ

Rabbanā ṣalli ʿalā man, ḥalla fī khayri 'l-biqāʿ

O our Lord! Send Your Blessings on the one who appeared in the best of all places.

(٦) أَنتَ غَوثُنَا جَمِيعًا   يَا مُجَمَّلَ الطِبَاعِ

Anta ghawthunā jamīʿan, yā mujammala 'ṭ-ṭibāʿ

You are the savior of us all, O You Who gathers all perfected character traits!

(٧) وَلَبِسنَا ثَوبَ عِزٍّ بَعدَ تَلفِيقِ الرِقَاعِ

Wa labisnā thawba ʿizzin, baʿda talfiqi 'r-riqāʿ

We were adorned with the robe of honor after patches and tatters.

(٨) أَسبِلِ السِّترَ عَلَينَا يَا مُجِيبًا كُلَّ دَاعى

Asbili 's-sitra ʿalaynā, yā mujīban kulla dāʿ

Cover us up our shortcomings, O Answerer of all requests!

(٩) وَصَلاَةُ الله عَلَى أَحمَدْ عَدَّ تَحرِيرِ الرِّقَاعِ

Wa ṣalātullāh ʿalā Āḥmad, ʿaddad taḥrīri 'r-riqāʿ

And Allāh's Blessing be upon Ahmad on the numbers of the freed lands!

(١٠) وكَذَا آلٍ وصَحبٍ مَا سَعَىْ للهِ سَاعِ

Wa kadhā ālin wa ṣaḥbin, mā saʿa li 'Llāhi sāʿ

And likewise, the Family and the Companions, as long as the striving is for Allāh!

Every such recitation and reading bears a share of staggering miracles and miraculous gifts. So, open your eyes and your hearts, and *inshā-Allāh* you shall find many things. Glory, praise and thanks be to Allāh, the Lord of the Worlds!

Celebrate the Most Noble Holy Qur'an!

Celebrate the Love of the Prophet ﷺ and his Companions! And Glory, praise and thanks be to Allāh, the Lord of the Worlds.

Duʿā, Supplication

اللَّهُمَّ اجْعَلْ أَوَّلَ سَنَتِنَا هَذَا صَلَاحًا وَأَوْسَطَهُ فَلَاحًا وَآخِرَهُ نَجَاحًا.

اللَّهُمَّ اجْعَلْ أَوَّلَهُ رَحْمَةً وَأَوْسَطَهُ نِعْمَةً وَآخِرَهُ تَكْرِمَةً وَمَغْفِرَةً.

Allāhuma ʼjʿal āwwal sannatinā hadhā ṣalāḥan wa awṣaṭahu falāḥan wa ākhirahu najāḥan. Allāhuma ʼjʿal āwwalahu raḥmatan wa awṣaṭahu niʿmatan wa ākhirahu takrīmatan wa maghfirah.

O our Lord! Make the beginning of this year goodness, its middle happiness, and its end success. O our Lord! Make its beginning mercy, its middle bounty and its ending generosity and forgiveness.

الحَمْدُ للهِ الَّذِى تَوَاضَعَ كُلُّ شَىْءٍ لِعَظَمَتِهِ وَذَلَّ كُلُّ شَىْءٍ لِعِزَّتِهِ وَخَضَعَ كُلُّ شَىْءٍ لِمُلْكِهِ وَاسْتَسْلَمَ كُلُّ شَىْءٍ لِقُدْرَتِهِ . وَالحَمْدُ للهِ الَّذِى سَكَنَ كُلُّ شَىْءٍ لِهَيْبَتِهِ وَأَظْهَرَ كُلَّ شَىْءٍ بِحِكْمَتِهِ وَتَصَاغَرَ كُلُّ شَىْءٍ لِكِبْرِيَائِهِ.

Alḥamdullilāhi ʼLladhī tawaḍʿa kullu shayin li-ʿaẓamatihi wa dhalla kullu shayin li-ʿizzatihi wa khaḍʿa kullu shayin li-mulkihi wʼastaslama kullu shayin li-qudratih. Alḥamdullilāhi ʼLladhī sakana kullu shayin li-haybatihi wa aẓhara kullu shayin bi-ḥikmatihi wa taṣāghara kullu shayin li-kibrīyāʼih.

All praise be to Allāh, Who humbled everything before His Greatness, made all things subservient before His Honor, brought low all things before His Kingship and made all things submit to His Power. And all praise to Allāh, Who made all things tranquil before His Majesty, and made everything appear through His Wisdom, and humbled all things before His Pride.

اللَّهُمَّ أَيْقِظْنَا فِى أَحَبِّ السَّاعَاتِ إِلَيْكَ يَا وَدُودُ يَا

Allāhuma 'ayqiẓnā fi aḥabbi's-saā'ti ilayk yā Wadūd, yā dha'l-'arshi'l-majīd fa'ālun limā yurīd.

O our Lord! Wake us in the time most beloved to Yourself, O Loving One, O Lord of the Throne of Glory, Doer (without let) of all that He intends.

يَا وَدُودُ يَا ﴿ذُو الْعَرْشِ الْمَجِيدُ فَعَّالٌ لِّمَا يُرِيدُ هَلْ أَتَاكَ حَدِيثُ الْجُنُودِ فِرْعَوْنَ وَثَمُودَ بَلِ الَّذِينَ كَفَرُوا فِى تَكْذِيبٍ وَاللهُ مِن وَرَائِهِم مُّحِيطٌ بَلْ هُوَ قُرْآنٌ مَّجِيدٌ فِى لَوْحٍ مَّحْفُوظٍ﴾

Yā Wadūd, yā dha 'l-'arshi 'l-majīd fa'ālun limā yurīd. Hal atāka ḥadīthu 'l-junūdi fira'wna wa thamūda bali 'Lladhīnā kafarū fi takdhībin w 'Allāhu min warā'ihim muḥīṭun bal huwa qurānun majīdun fī lawḥin maḥfūẓ.

O Loving One, O "*Has the story reached you, of the forces of Pharaoh and the Thamūd? And yet the Unbelievers (persist) in rejecting (the Truth), while*

Allāh encompasses them from behind! But, this is a Glorious Qur'an, (Inscribed) in a Tablet Preserved!"[6]

اللَّهُمَّ اغْفِرْ لِى ذُنُوبِى وَلِوَالِدَىّ كَمَا رَبّيَانِى صَغِيرًا وَ لِجَمِيعِ الْمُؤمِنِينَ وَ الْمُؤمِنَات، وَالْمسْلِمِينَ وَ الْمسْلِمَات، اَللأحيَاءِ مِنهُم وَ اَلأَمْوَات، وَاغْفِرْ لَنَا وَلإِخْوَانِنَا الَّذِينَ سَبَقُونَا بِالْإِيمَانِ وَلَا تَجْعَلْ فِى قُلُوبِنَا غِلاَّ لِّلَّذِينَ آمَنُوا رَبَّنَا إِنَّكَ رَؤُوفٌ رَّحِيمٌ يَا أَرحَمَ الرَاحِمِين

Allāhuma 'ghfir lī dhunūbī wa li-wālidayya kamā rabbayānī ṣaghīra wa li-jamīʿi 'l-mūminīna wa 'l-mūmināti wa 'l-muslimīna wa 'l-muslimāti al-aḥyā'i minhum wa 'l-amwāt wa 'ghfir lanā wa li-ikhwāninā 'Lladhīna sabaqūna bi 'l-īmāni wa lā tajʿal fī qulūbanā ghillan li 'Lladhīna āmanū rabbanā innaka rā'ūfun raḥīmun yā arḥama 'r-rāḥimīn.

O Allāh! Forgive me my sins and my parents' just as they raised me when I was small and to all the Believers, men and women, and all the Muslims, men and women, both the living among them and the dead. And *"Forgive us and our brethren who came before us into the Faith and leave not in our hearts rancor against those who have believed. Our Lord! You*

---

[6] Sūratu 'l-Buruj, 85:15-22.

are indeed Full of Kindness, Most Merciful."[7] O Most Merciful of those who show mercy!

وَ صَلَى اَللهُ عَلَى سَيدِنَا وَ نَبيِينَا مُحَمَدٍ وَ عَلَى أَلِهِ وَ صَحْبِهِ أَجْمَعْين. سُبْحَانَ رَبّكَ رَبِّ الْعِزَّةِ عَمَّا يَصِفُونَ وَسَلَامٌ عَلَى الْمُرْسَلِينَ وَالْحَمْدُ لِلَّهِ رَبِّ الْعَالَمِينَ رَبَنَا تَقبَل مِنّا بِحُرمَةِ مَن أَنزَلتَ عَليهِ سِرسُورَةِ الفَاتِحَة.

Wa ṣalla 'Llāhu ʿalā Sayyīdīnā wa Nabīyyīnā Muḥammadin wa ʿalā ālihi wa ṣaḥbihi ajmaʿīn. Subḥāna Rabbika Rabbi 'l-ʿizzati ʿammā yaṣifūn wa salāmun ʿalā 'l-mursalīn wa 'l-ḥamdulillāh Rabbi 'l-ʿālamīn. Rabbanā taqabbal minnā bi-ḥurmati man anzalta ʿalayhi sirri sūratu 'l-Fātiḥa!

Blessings upon our Master, Prophet Muḥammad and upon his Family and all his Companions. Glory be to our Lord, the Lord of Power, above what they describe! And peace be upon the Messengers. Praise belongs to God, the Lord of the Worlds. O our Lord! Accept from us for the sake of the one on whom You revealed the secrets of the Opening Chapter of the Holy Qur'an, al-Fātiḥa!

Shaykh Muhammad Hisham Kabbani
19 August 2020/1 Muḥarram 1442
Fenton, Michigan

---

[7] Sūratu 'l-Ḥashr, 59:1.

الله

Greatness of the Holy Qur'an

The Eternal, Living Divine Favor

A'ūdhu billāhi min ash-shayṭāni 'r-rajīm.

Bismillāhi 'r-Raḥmāni 'r-Raḥīm.

Allāh ﷻ bestowed *Ummat an-Nabī* ﷺ with an important favor, one that He ﷻ did not grant to any other nation. It is a living favor, eternal, with no expiry date or limits, whereas everything else has limits, comes and goes, and has no lasting existence. Whatever favor Allāh ﷻ grants from His Will that doesn't come and go and is always present is a living favor.

Today, whatever we do has an end, but the Living Favor is Divine and has no beginning and no end. Unfortunately, we don't keep the importance of that Living Favor in our hearts; we forget about it, sometimes we remember, sometimes we don't.

It is said, اجلّ الكرمات دوام التوفيق *ajalla al-karamāt dawām at-tawfīq*, "The best of miracles is the continuity of what you are doing," especially something that lives forever.

So, if you keep doing that good deed even a little bit, as Allāh ﷻ said:

لَا يُكَلِّفُ ٱللَّهُ نَفْسًا إِلَّا وُسْعَهَا ۚ لَهَا مَا كَسَبَتْ وَعَلَيْهَا مَا ٱكْتَسَبَتْ

> *On no soul does Allāh place a burden greater than it can bear. It gets every good that it earns, and it suffers every ill that it earns.*[8]

Even if you do a small portion from that Living Favor, it is as if you have done the whole requirement! And He did not give that favor to any other nation, such as to Sayyīdinā Nūḥ عليه السلام, Sayyīdinā Ibrāhīm عليه السلام, Sayyīdinā Mūsā عليه السلام, Sayyīdinā ʿIsa عليه السلام, none of the main prophets. What Allāh ﷻ gave to us through Sayyīdinā Muḥammad ﷺ, is Eternal! What He gave to the other prophets was for their time and then stopped, but what He gave to Sayyīdinā Muḥammad ﷺ is continuous.

So, what did Allāh ﷻ give? It is a favor that contains the secret of all of Creation! What He gave is not created, but every Creation He created is contained within that Divine Favor!

All prophets, especially Sayyīdinā Mūsā عليه السلام, asked, "*Yā Rabbī*! Give me something that You did not give to anyone else," but Allāh ﷻ said, "No, that is only for My Beloved Prophet Muḥammad ﷺ!"

Sayyīdinā Sulaymān عليه السلام was clever. He said, "O Allāh! Give me *mulk*, a kingdom that no one can

---

[8] Sūratu 'l-Baqarah, 2:286.

have after me." So, Allāh ﷻ gave, and Sayyīdinā Sulaymān ﷺ conquered *dunyā*, but it is now gone.

For the Prophet ﷺ, Allāh ﷻ didn't give only *dunyā*, but He also gave *Ākhirah*, which is everlasting and does not expire, a Divine, Living Favor for *Ummat an-Nabī* ﷺ that never ends!

Allāh ﷻ favored the Prophet ﷺ and his *Ummah* above all other prophets, as everything they were given expired, except for Islam and the Holy Qur'an.

Allāh ﷻ said:

إِنَّ الدِّينَ عِندَ اللهِ الإِسْلاَمُ

Inna 'd-dīna ʿinda 'Llāhi 'l-Islām

Indeed, the religion in the sight of Allāh is Islam.[9]

He didn't say, *"Inna 'd-dīna ʿinda 'Llāhi 't-Tawrāt aw Banī Israīl."* The Holy Qur'an contains everything that came before and everything that will come after, as it is Allāh's Holy Words. The *Tawrāt*, Torah, and the *Injīl*, Bible, are human words written more than a hundred years after the revelation of the Holy Qur'an; they are collections, but the Holy Qur'an is not a collection. As it was revealed it remains the same today, letter for letter!

---

[9] Sūrat Āli-ʿImrān, 3:19.

Open the Book with Faith

Everyone has hundreds, even thousands of books. Go to libraries and you will find millions of books have been written. Can any book in this world pay you back? No, you spend your money and then you put it on the shelf. The only book that gives back to you when you read it, and even after you read it and when you put it on the shelf, is the Holy Qur'an. The presence of Holy Qur'an in the house will give you healing (*shifā'*), because it is Allāh's Words! If you are sick, open the Holy Qur'an!

الْفَاتِحَةُ لِمَا قُرِئَتْ لَهُ

The Prophet ﷺ said in a *Ḥadīth ash-Sharīf*:

> *(The Benefit of) the Chapter of The Opening (Sūratu 'l-Fātiḥa) is for whatever it is read.*[10]

Sūratu 'l-Fātiḥa will cure you from any sickness you have, but to do so, you must have belief in the Holy Qur'an, in what you are reciting, and your breath must be clean—not just breath that is clean from brushing your teeth when you prepare to read—but you must have no bad behaviors or

---

[10] Gloss of a statement by the Successor 'Atā: "Whoever has a need should recite the Opening of the Book up to its end, and it will be fulfilled by Allah's Will." (Abū Shaykh)

manners in order for the prayer (*duʿā*) you read through the Holy Qur'an to be effective.

That is why sometimes people go to see a pious person and say, "Make *duʿā* for me!" That is not associating partners with Allāh (*shirk*). Everyone accepts that such petitions on your behalf are valid, but there are conditions for your own *duʿā* to be accepted:

وَنُنَزِّلُ مِنَ الْقُرْآنِ مَا هُوَ شِفَاء وَرَحْمَةٌ لِّلْمُؤْمِنِينَ وَلاَ يَزِيدُ الظَّالِمِينَ إَلاَّ خَسَارًا

> *And We sent down in the Qur'an such things that have healing and mercy for the Believers (Mu'minīn), but it does not increase the wrongdoers (ẓālimīn) except in loss.*[11]

Who is Allāh ﷻ addressing in this verse? The believers (*Mu'min*). He gives a cure from Holy Qur'an, but for an oppressor (*ẓālim*), he is making them to be in loss (*khasāra*). Who is Allāh ﷻ addressing? The *kuffār*, unbelievers? No, He is not addressing a *kāfir*. He is addressing us, saying: "If you believe in the Verses of My Holy Qur'an, which is My Word, then you are a *Mu'min,* believer, and you will be cured."

However, if you are a *ẓālim*, oppressor to others, how are you going to see results? And there are

---

[11] Sūratu 'l-Isrā', 17:82.

many oppressors among Muslims, who, though they believe in Qur'an, are *ẓālim* to the Holy Qur'an because their manners are unclean, and they are oppressive to their own souls. They are opening the Holy Qur'an in a state of cruelty, so Allāh ﷻ is saying, "Be a *Mu'min,* have faith in what you are reading, then you will see the results." If you have no faith, how are you going to see results?

Etiquettes of Reading and Handling the Holy Qur'an

Everything in this World is Based on Good Manners

Aʿūdhu billāhi min ash-shayṭāni 'r-rajīm.

Bismillāhi 'r-Raḥmāni 'r-Raḥīm.

Every action we do has to coincide with what Allāh ﷻ likes, and every speech we give must correspond to what the Prophet ﷺ likes. Also, every matter that concerns us in *dunyā* has to be accepted through *Shariʿah*; we cannot do something rejected by *Shariʿah*, and that is the true *adab*, proper manners. We use *adab* in many matters, and everything has its own proper conduct. For example, you cannot put the Holy Qur'an on the table upside down; it must be facing upwards so *Sūratu 'l-Fātiḥa* is at the top. *Adab* for Holy Qur'an is in how you carry it and that you do not put it on the floor.

Everything has its etiquette. In your prayers, showing etiquette means to cut out all bad gossips that come into the mind as much as possible. Speaking to others in a nice way is also *adab*. So, everything in *dunyā* is based on *adab*, good manners.

Take the Holy Qur'an on Your Head as a Crown

The Holy Qur'an is Allāh's Words, not anyone else's words. May Allāh ﷻ make us to love the Holy Qur'an more and to read it more.

O Muslims and non-Muslims! The Holy Qur'an is a book, but it was not created. It was compiled by the *Ṣaḥābah* ؓ. They heard and saw the Revelation; they saw what we did not see. The Prophet ﷺ lived that Revelation and no one else did. He gave that Revelation the sweetness from his holy mouth. He read it in a holy way, and no one heard it but the *Ṣaḥābah,* and they passed it on by compiling it as a book.

The Words that were revealed carry an infinite number of secrets that Allāh ﷻ revealed to His Prophet ﷺ! If this entire *dunyā* becomes pens and all the oceans become ink, then what Allāh ﷻ is giving to Prophet ﷺ now will not be finished, and what Allāh ﷻ is giving to Prophet ﷺ out of His Holy Words from the beginning until now is but a drop of what He ﷻ has yet to give.

O Muslims! Take the Light of Qur'an and its benefit as a crown. If you do not read it, put the Holy Qur'an on your head every day and let its Light penetrate your whole body and nervous system. It will affect you and make you strong and powerful on that day. But what are we doing? We are putting the Holy Qur'an in a cabinet and saying, "We have benefit."

In some countries, like Indonesia and in some Arab countries, they sew a cover for the Holy Qur'an and hang it in their homes for *barakah,* a blessing. Here, I never saw the Holy Qur'an hung as it is back home. You see people here in the mosques reading the Qur'an, and when they finish, they put it on the floor! That is not *adab*, as then their feet are higher than the Holy Qur'an when they pray. The Holy Qur'an must be on your head! Anyone who gives respect to the Holy Qur'an, Allāh ﷻ will give respect to them on the Day of Judgment, and anyone who disrespects the Holy Qur'an, Allāh will disrespect them on the Day of Judgment.

May Allāh ﷻ forgive us and grant us to be among those who respect Holy Qur'an.

Respect Holy Qur'an's Teachings by Helping the Poor

They used to compete in Lebanon on who can complete reading the Holy Qur'an before others, and this is from the blessing of the Prophet ﷺ.

It is not permissible for anyone to put the Holy Qur'an aside unless they are sick, or they are traveling. Today, as we said, we leave the Holy Qur'an on a shelf, not reading from it. There is no more respect for Allāh's Word!

One of the highest ranking shaykhs and *Awlīyā* used to always respect the Holy Qur'an, placing it on top of the highest shelf so that it is at the highest point in his house. Nowadays, we put the Holy Qur'an on the lowest level possible and use it only as a decoration.

This *Walī* was very rich; he built his house on a cliff and invited people to his house. He was one of the best *murīds*, disciples, of his shaykh. He built his house on top of the cliff and placed the Holy Qur'an at the highest point in the house, to show highest respect to the Qur'an, and he presented the reward of doing that as a donation for his shaykh in order for the other *murīds* to see and respect the Holy Qur'an. He used to say, "The love of the Qur'an is in my heart!"

The Shaykh was very happy with the respect that *murid* showed the Qur'an, and the *murīd* was very happy at his shaykh's acceptance, so he went and bought another copy of the Holy Qur'an and placed it higher than the first. He then went to his shaykh's house to tell him this good news, that he had made a new place at the topmost point of his house to put the Holy Qur'an and he presented that Qur'an to his shaykh as a gift. The shaykh was very happy that the *murīd* was respecting his teachings and respecting the reading of the Holy Qurʿan.

However, the shaykh then asked, "Did you rest well?" His asking this was a subtle indication that there is something wrong, meaning, "Did you think about it?" Out of humility the *murīd* answered, "No, I didn't listen to what the Holy Qur'an gave to human beings," meaning, he did not feel he had shown the highest respect to the Message of the Qur'an. The shaykh was teaching him a lesson, saying, "I accept the Holy Qur'an you gave me, but I give it back to you, because it is a big responsibility to carry it if you don't respect it perfectly."

That *murīd* was shaking, he did not know what to answer. So, he left the Qur'an in the house of the shaykh and left. After a while, someone came and gave the Qur'an back to the *murīd*. The shaykh said to the *murīd,* "You are the best *murīd* in the group, but you did something that the Prophet ﷺ did not like." What was that? The shaykh told him, "I accept your gift, but you have to know that I do not like to see powerful, rich people leaving those in need without help. Don't sleep on your money, without supporting the sick or the needy!" There are a lot of people today who have no shelter; they have nothing in their homes, everything has been destroyed and no one is responding to their cries!

So, the generous must always remember the poor. We have to help the people in need. What does it mean to help the people in need? It means, you have to always remember at any moment you could lose all your good deeds due to something wrong you did. So, please make sure to help, and this is the time for helping!

The shaykh was happy when his *murīd* gave a good answer. He said that if you bring all the gold and wealth of *dunyā* and put it in front of *Awlīyāullāh,* they will not look at it for even one moment as much as they look at the rest of the *Awlīyā* and at poor people! The shaykh said, "If you only knew that the heaviness and the burdens of *dunyā* do not end! However, you will not understand anything, but *alḥamdulillāh* at least you have shown good respect to the Holy Qur'an."

We are Muslims and our Book is the Holy Qur'an, so make sure you give as much as you can, as Allāh ﷻ said in the Holy Qur'an:

الٓمٓ ﴿١﴾ ذَٰلِكَ ٱلْكِتَابُ لَا رَيْبَ ۛ فِيهِ ۛ هُدًى لِّلْمُتَّقِينَ ﴿٢﴾

ٱلَّذِينَ يُؤْمِنُونَ بِٱلْغَيْبِ وَيُقِيمُونَ ٱلصَّلَوٰةَ وَمِمَّا رَزَقْنَاهُمْ يُنفِقُونَ ﴿٣﴾

Alif. Lām. Mīm. Dhālika 'l-kitābu lā rayba fīhi hudal-li 'l-muttaqīn. Alladhīna yu'minūna bi 'l-ghaybi wa yuqīmūna 'ṣ-ṣalāta <u>*wa mimmā razaqnāhum yunfiqūn.*</u>

Alif. Lām. Mīm.

This is the Book about which there is no doubt, a Guidance for those conscious of Allāh, who believe

> *in the Unseen, establish prayer and spend out of what We have provided for them.*[12]

People don't have roofs on their homes; they don't have food, and *mashāAllāh* we have everything! So, we have to be careful not to become disillusioned from *Ākhirah* by the attraction of *dunyā*.

الدنيا جيفة وطلابها كلاب

It is said, "This *dunyā* is dirt and filth, and those who seek it are dogs."[13]

You have to build a relationship between yourself and other people who are in need so they too can live a good life.

Alḥamdulillāh, all praise is to Allāh! *Alḥamdulillāh*, we thank you, O Allāh, for granting us the ability to recite "*Alḥamdulillāh*," with a praise that is the praise of the Prophet ﷺ and a praise that is worthy of Your Majesty!

May Allāh ﷻ grant us what He granted His *Awlīyāullāh*, because we are in His *Maḥabbah*, Love: we love Sayyīdinā *Rasūlullāh* ﷺ, we love *Awlīyāullāh*, and we love each other.

---

[12] Sūratu 'l-Baqarah, 2:1-3.

[13] Abū Shaykh and Abu Na'īm al-Asbahānī as a saying of 'Alī ibn Abī Ṭālib ؓ, considered extremely weak or forged.

Until today, there is this blessing of *ḥamd*, praise, a praise that befits Your Blessings and Your Bounties, abundant and a clear praise. So, you must think, "What can I do to make Allāh ﷻ, the Prophet ﷺ and *Awlīyāullāh* happy with me?" Everyone must help! And those who do not have anything, their help is by saying, "*Alḥamdulillāhi Rabbi 'l-'ālamīn*, all praise is due to Allāh, Lord of the Worlds."[14] We praise Him and thank Him for His Gifts and His Bounties, the outward and the inward.

Five Signs of a True Believer

Grandshaykh 'AbdAllāh, may Allāh bless his soul, once asked, "What are the signs or descriptions of a dervish?" For example, in this meeting we said to take out your beads and make *tasbīḥ*. You have to always be ready and prepared, as when you travel in the desert or jungle you don't know what wild animals will attack you, so you carry a knife out of fear.

Shayṭān can attack you at any time, therefore in order to prevent his attacks you must carry these five signs on you. Thus, when a *Walī* looks at you, he knows if you are a dervish or not.

[14] Sūratu 'l-Fātiḥa, 1:4.

The first sign is you must always have the Holy Qur'an with you, if not by memorizing, then by keeping your tongue wet with *Dhikrullāh*.

عَنْ عَبْدِ اللَّهِ بْنِ بُسْرٍ، رضى الله عنه أَنَّ رَجُلاً، قَالَ يَا رَسُولَ اللَّهِ إِنَّ شَرَائِعَ الإِسْلاَمِ قَدْ كَثُرَتْ عَلَىَّ فَأَخْبِرْنِى بِشَىْءٍ أَتَشَبَّثُ بِهِ . قَالَ " لاَ يَزَالُ لِسَانُكَ رَطْبًا مِنْ ذِكْرِ اللَّهِ " . الترمذى.

A man once came to the Prophet ﷺ and said:

> *"Yā Rasūlullāh! The rules of Islam became heavy on me, so give me news of something which I can maintain."*
>
> *The Prophet ﷺ said, "Make your tongue wet with Dhikrullāh."*[15]

The first *Dhikrullāh* is the Holy Qur'an, so you must have the Holy Qur'an to be considered a dervish. Whether you read aloud or do *Dhikrullāh* silently, the angels will come, for they hear you; if you recite aloud, they hear you and if you recite silently, they hear you even more, as silent recitation has more *barakah*.

وَاذْكُر رَّبَّكَ فِى نَفْسِكَ تَضَرُّعًا وَخِيفَةً وَدُونَ الْجَهْرِ مِنَ الْقَوْلِ بِالْغُدُوِّ وَالآصَالِ وَلاَ تَكُن مِّنَ الْغَافِلِينَ

---

[15] Tirmidhī.

> *And remember your Lord within yourself in humility and in reverence, without loudness in words, in the mornings and evenings. And do not be among the heedless.*[16]

Allāh ﷻ is saying, "Recite that *Dhikr* very silently when you go out in the daytime and in the evening," as Allāh ﷻ does not like someone showing off: "Look, I am reading Holy Qur'an!" or, "I am doing *Dhikrullāh*!" So, keep a low profile.

إِنَّا نَحْنُ نَزَّلْنَا الذِّكْرَ وَإِنَّا لَهُ لَحَافِظُونَ

> *Truly We have revealed the Remembrance, and truly We protect it.*[17]

The one reciting Holy Qur'an will be *ḥāfiẓ*, kept by Allāh ﷻ, protected by the Holy Qur'an. The *Ḥuffāẓ* (memorizers of Qur'an) will be shining like lamps on the Day of Judgment because they memorized Allāh's Ancient Words! How great they are a *barakah,* blessing, among us! So, don't let your children leave off memorizing the Holy Qur'an! If they do not memorize the entire Qur'an, at least they can read the Holy Qur'an and make the *khatm*, completion, but don't drop reading of the Holy Qur'an, leaving it on the shelves.

---

[16] Sūratu 'l-'Araf, 7:205.

[17] Sūratu 'l-Ḥijr, 15:9.

You may recite *Sūratu 'l-Ikhlāṣ* up to 1,000 times daily, as such a one is carrying the Holy Qur'an. You cannot carry the Holy Qur'an to work and back, but you can recite *"Qul Hūw Allāhu Āḥad..."* or whichever *sūrah* you have memorized. Now people listen to *qasīdahs* when driving, which is nice, but why not put on the Holy Qur'an? Then you will memorize while coming and going.

So, the first sign of a dervish, a simple person standing at the Door of the Prophet ﷺ and the Door of Allāh ﷻ, is to have *Dhikrullāh* of *"Lā ilāha illa 'Llah Muḥammadun Rasūlullāh"* on top of your head, especially for Muslims. We are not speaking about non-Muslims. Every Muslim will have *Dhikrullāh* written on his head, and if he is not keeping it, that *"Lā ilāha illa 'Llah Muḥammadun Rasūlullāh"* will fade. Then, *Awlīyāullāh* will say, "What happened to this person? *'Lā ilāha illa 'Llah Muḥammadun Rasūlullāh'* was written, but now it is faded," which means he neglected his *awrād*. *Dhikrullāh* is not the same as a lecture or advice, about which the Prophet ﷺ said, *"Ad-dīnu nasīḥa, Religion is advice."* That does not take you higher like *Dhikrullāh* does. If you say, *"Lā ilāha illa 'Llah"* once, it takes you to Paradise.

عَنِ الزُّهْرِيِّ أَنَّهُ سُئِلَ عَنْ قَوْلِ النَّبِيِّ صلى الله عليه وسلم " مَنْ قَالَ لاَ إِلَهَ إِلاَّ اللَّهُ دَخَلَ الْجَنَّةَ "

The Prophet ﷺ said:

> *Whoever says "Lā ilāha illa 'Llah" enters Paradise.*[18]

If angels see *"Lā ilāha illa 'Llah Muḥammadun Rasūlullāh"* written on your forehead, they know you are from *adh-dhākirūn*, the remembering ones. That is why *Dhikrullāh* is recommended in different *ṭarīqahs*; they do *jahrī Dhikr* (aloud) as they want others to hear it. Some, like Naqshbandis, do silent *Dhikr* according to the *āyah* we mentioned earlier. But first, you must prepare yourself for *Dhikrullāh*. How can we be clean? You have to recite *Dalā'il al-Khayrāt* to prepare for Reality, and Reality is not related to how much you possess of this *dunyā*.

Muḥammad at-Talmaysānī ق, was one of the pious servants. Once he completed reading *Dalā'il al-Khayrāt* 100,000 times and gifted its reward to the Prophet ﷺ. He saw the Prophet ﷺ in his dream, telling him, "I will give you a *Ṣalawāt* equal to reciting *Dalā'il al-Khayrāt* 800,000 times." He recited it without awareness of what he got, but then the Prophet ﷺ rewarded him 800,000 times more![19]

وَأْتُوا الْبُيُوتَ مِنْ أَبْوَابِهَا

---

[18] Tirmidhī.

[19] The *ṣalawāt* taught by the Prophet ﷺ to Muḥammad at-Talmaysānī is known as *Ṣalawāt al-Fāṭih*.

Approach houses from their doors.[20]

The Arabic word *buyūt,* houses, has many meanings. Here it means "come to your destiny through the door," meaning, "come to what you accomplished through the door assigned to you." Our door is through the Prophet ﷺ. To get to *Dhikrullāh,* you must open the door by means of *Ṣalawāt,* prayers upon the Prophet ﷺ.

To be a real dervish, you must recite *Ṣalawāt* 1,000 to 24,000 times a day. You may be busy working but your heart is busy, and you must continuously make *Dhikrullāh* and *Ṣalawāt* without interruption. A dervish who gave himself to Allāh ﷻ can simultaneously do his *Dhikrullāh,* *Ṣalawāt* and his work, because he does not say, "I am dedicating one hour to read Holy Qur'an or *Ṣalawāt;*" rather, he is continuously diving in the ocean of Holy Qur'an and *Ṣalawāt,* so his body is continuously like that.

لِى سَاعةٌ مَع الرَّب وَسَاعةٌ مَع الخَلْق

As the Prophet ﷺ said:

I have one image, one side (or one hour) with my Lord and one side (or one hour) with the people.[21]

---

[20] Sūratu 'l-Baqarah, 2:189.

[21] *Risālat al-Qushayrīyya,* with no chain.

So, the dervish who is with Allāh ﷻ will find a lot of time, as his whole body becomes *dhākir*, always in remembrance! Like the wind keeps a fan running, similarly that dervish will have a wind that makes his heart running in *Dhikrullāh* and, therefore, it does not interrupt his work. At that time, you begin to do *Ṣalawāt* and according to how strong that *Ṣalawāt* is, you will be assigned a door. That will be your door on Judgment Day, your door when you go to your grave, and your door in *dunyā*!

Awlīyāullāh can detect your door and they assign *awrād* to *murīds*. That is assigned to the *murīd* by the Prophet ﷺ through his guiding *Walī*. Be sure not to jump from one *Walī* to another, because then no door will open for you; that *Walī* you follow is a door that takes you to the Prophet ﷺ and from him ﷺ to Allāh ﷻ.

The beginner who wants to enter into the guidance of *Shuyūkh al-Kummal*, Perfected Shaykhs, must take the permission to read the Holy Qur'an from the shaykh as part of the *awrād*, daily devotions for blessings. That is why they tell you to read one *juz* (part) of Holy Qur'an daily and not to miss it, unless you are traveling, you have guests, or you are sick. Then, they are able to witness for you, making sure that it is written for you, presenting you in the presence of the Prophet ﷺ and to the Divine Presence, where the Prophet ﷺ says, "*Yā Rabbī, hādhā min ummatī*, O my Lord!

This one from my *Ummah* has read the Holy Qur'an!" When you take that certification of authenticity through *adab*, good conduct, then you will never be heedless! You will become more and more wise. This is especially true for young ones, as they can read and memorize easily, not like the elderly who can no longer memorize.

So, first you have the Holy Qur'an with you, either by memorizing or by reading from the physical book, or by reciting *Sūratu 'l-Ikhlāṣ*, then *Dalā'il al-Khayrāt, Ṣalāt al-Ibrāhīmīyya,* or any popular *Ṣalawāt* that everyone knows. That will guide you to your door, which once it opens, never closes, as in video games: you go to one level and a door opens, then you go to another stage.

As you are approaching the Divine Level of the Prophet ﷺ, when that door opens do not expect it to become easy, no! They want to see how patient you are, maintaining your *awrād* in your normal life and keeping *wāridāt,* inspirations that come to your heart and following what you must in order to ascend higher and higher. It becomes so painful, because it seems you are going to reach the goal and when you come closer to reaching that horizon, then you see another horizon! When *Awlīyāullāh* begin to dive in the love of Sayyīdinā Muḥammad ﷺ, they find that difficulty.

Sometimes people say, "When we do *awrād,* we feel heavy," because the more doors they open, the stronger the power becomes. For example, it is not like 100 volts, 240 volts or 360 volts, but rather it is like the strongest voltage coming directly from a transformer.

So, when we do *Dhikrullāh,* sometimes it comes heavy on the chest. When that happens, make *Ṣalawāt,* that is a cleaning process. *Ṣalawāt* on the Prophet ﷺ is very recommended, because *Asmā'u 'Llah al-Ḥusnā,* Allāh's Beautiful Names and Attributes carry a lot of majestic power that sometimes people cannot carry. That is why in Mecca, *ṣalāt* is equal to 100,000 times, but in *Madīnatu 'l-Munawwarah,* it is equal to 24,000 times, it is reduced.

So, two signs you have to carry are the Holy Qur'an and *Dalā'il al-Khayrāt.*

The third prerequisite of *dervish*-hood is *wuḍū,* ablution, as it is said, "*Al-wuḍū ṣilāḥ al-mu'min,* the ablution is the weapon of the Believer."

The fourth prerequisite is using the *miswāk* (toothstick from the Arak/Neem tree) to come pure to prayer and worship.

عَنْ أَبِى هُرَيْرَةَ، قَالَ قَالَ رَسُولُ اللَّهِ - ﷺ " لَوْلاَ أَنْ أَشُقَّ عَلَى أُمَّتِى لأَمَرْتُهُمْ بِالسِّوَاكِ عِنْدَ كُلِّ صَلاَةٍ " .

The Prophet ﷺ said:

Had I not thought it difficult for my Ummah, I would have commanded them to use the miswāk (tooth-stick) before every prayer.[22]

Using the *miswāk* before prayer increases its value 27 times. Also, use it before beginning *Dhikrullāh* as a means to repel Shayṭān's attacks. Just as ablution is needed to protect your prayers, you must have a physical means to repel Shayṭān when carrying the physical Holy Qur'an and the physical *Dalā'il al-Khayrāt*.

Grandshaykh ق relates that one time the unbelievers attacked, and the Prophet ﷺ ordered the Companions ؓ to take out their *miswāk*, sit on the ground, raise one knee and lean on it, then recite:

اَللّٰهُمَّ طَهِر قَلْبِى مِنْ الشِرْكِ وَالنِفَاق

Allāhumma ṭahhir qalbī min ash-shirki wa 'n-nifāq.

O Allāh! Purify my heart of polytheism and hypocrisy.

Doing this, purifies us from hidden *shirk,* because gossips are always coming to our hearts as we constantly download bad information into our heart's "chip." Therefore, purify it by using *miswāk*.

---

[22] Ibn Mājah, from Abū Hurayrah ؓ.

Finally, you also need to carry with you a prayer rug in order that you are always ready for your prayers.

So, these are the five things you need to carry with you at all times, which are the signs of a real *Mu'min,* Believer: (1) The Holy Qur'an, (2) *Dalā'il al-Khayrāt,* (3) *miswāk,* (4) a prayer rug, and (5) *wuḍū.*

May Allāh ﷻ make our every breath in and out to be in *Dhikrullāh,* with *wuḍū* and with *Ṣalawāt* on the Prophet ﷺ. But don't think sitting in a corner doing *Dhikrullāh* makes you a dervish! No, to be dervish is to recite the Holy Qur'an and *Dalā'il al-Khayrāt* while you are working, like people listen to music with earphones, so why not listen to Holy Qur'an?

Awlīyāullāh recommend listening to the Holy Qur'an whenever you can, because slowly, slowly your body will react to it by itself and you will begin to hear your heart saying, "*Allāh, Allāh...! Hūwa, Hūwa...!*" Then, as soon as you put your tongue on the roof of your mouth, your heart will begin to move; as soon as you hold the beads to make *Dhikrullāh,* your *Shahādah* finger will move! The importance is not the beads, the importance is to move the *Shahādah* finger. At first it will interrupt your work, but gradually it will no longer do so; it will take you to the River of

Paradise, then out to the ocean, where the fish are living, and they don't drown.

SubḥānAllāh! May Allāh forgive us and accept from us.

الله

Secrets of the Holy Qur’an

The Unimaginable Benefits of Reading the Holy Qur’an

Aʿūdhu billāhi min ash-shayṭāni 'r-rajīm.

Bismillāhi 'r-Raḥmāni 'r-Raḥīm.

Al-qur'ānu nāṭiqun, "The Holy Qur'an utters, speaks," it is a Talking Book." If you really have ears that can hear what cannot be heard, when you read verses from the Holy Qur’an, you will hear what they are saying and they will answer you. If you come across a Verse of Punishment, it will address you, saying, "You have these sins and this is the punishment you will get, so quickly repent!" You will hear that! If you come across Verses of Paradise, they will tell you, "You did this and this. Do more and you will reach higher Paradises!"

The holy letters and verses of the Qur’an are alive; the Holy Qur’an is alive! When you are reading the letters, what kind of realities do they open? What kind of knowledge these letter or words in the Holy Qur'an are speaking to you? What kind of knowledge oceans are these letters hiding?

When I read them, it is as if I am hearing them and listening to them, but the question is: what are they saying and what kind of realities are they opening?

It came to my heart that one of these letters sends heavenly rays of light; you can feel it and see it coming from the Holy Qur'an. That is why we say the Holy Qur'an is not silent; it speaks, and its language is Arabic.

The Holy Qur'an has no limits, and that is why people are recommended to read it, especially Muslims. Non-Muslims may not be able to read it because it is in Arabic, but otherwise, it is good to make *Dhikrullāh,* Divine Remembrance and to try to learn to read. It is permitted to read in English, but if we know Arabic, it is better and recommended, as the Arabic language is *barakah,* a blessing.

I used to hear every time from Grandshaykh ʿAbdAllāh ق, may Allāh bless his soul, that immediately after *āyātu 'l-ʿadhāb,* verses of punishment in the Holy Qur'an, come *āyātu 'r-raḥmah,* verses of mercy. This is to balance, because an *ʿabd,* a servant has to be worried and afraid, but when he is afraid, Allāh ﷻ immediately sends him a verse of *raḥmah,* mercy! That is why He ﷻ said in the Holy Qur'an:

وَمَا نُرْسِلُ بِالآيَاتِ إِلاَّ تَخْوِيفًا

We send not the Signs except as a warning.[23]

"We do not send verses except to scare you." In the hidden meaning, it means, "We are happy with you; Our *Raḥmah,* Mercy is there to take care of you and balance what you are afraid of, but you must be ready!"

Grandshaykh ق used to explain that Allāh ﷻ gave a specialty in the Holy Qur'an that whenever someone reads a verse of punishment, he or she will immediately be dressed from the secret that verse carries, and all the punishment will be removed from that person! So, every verse of *ʿadhāb,* punishment, cleans you from inside, leaving you free of any kind of punishment on the Day of Judgment. And similarly, every verse and word relating to Paradise, forgiveness or mercy will dress you with these manifestations of Allāh's Mercy and Forgiveness!

Ignite the Light in Your Heart with Holy Letters

What is the first letter in the Arabic alphabet? *Alif* (ا). It is always *shāmikha,* standing, uprising. The second letter *Bā* (ب) is always in *sajda;* it is a

---

[23] Sūratu 'l-Isrā, 17:59.

horizontal *Alif*, but prostrating to the standing *Alif*! Why did the *Bā* come after *Alif*? *Alif* is the first letter in "Allāh" and the *Bā* represents the Prophet ﷺ, who is in complete *sajda*, prostration.

When the first revelation came to the Prophet ﷺ, Jibrīl ☷ said to him, "*Yā*, Muḥammad, *iqrā'*, read!" and the Prophet ﷺ asked, "What am I going to read?" and Jibrīl ☷ said, "*Bismi* (بسم), in the Name of," the *Bā* being the first letter to read.

The opening of this universe is by the letter *Bā* in the name "*Bi* (بِ)"; it's the *Bā* (ب) that came after, and is continuously in *sajda*, prostration, to the *Alif*, to Allāh. Allāh ﷻ is saying, "*Bi-Ismī*, call Me by My Names: In the Name of Allāh, *ar-Raḥmān ar-Raḥīm*, the Most Merciful, the Compassionate!"

There are three Beautiful Names and three *Mīms* (م) in "*Bismillāhi 'r-Raḥmāni 'r-Raḥīm*." The first *Mīm* is in "*Bismi* (بسم)," the second *Mīm* is in "*Ar-Raḥmān* (الرحمن)," and the third is in "*Ar-Raḥīm* (الرحيْم)," each *Mīm* representing Muḥammad (محمد), Āḥmad (احمد), Maḥmūd (محمود)! Allāh ﷻ gave the Prophet ﷺ one name on Earth, Muḥammad ﷺ, and two names in Heavens, Ahmad ﷺ and Maḥmūd ﷺ.

That is only to give us an idea about the Greatness of Allāh ﷻ and the meanings you can extract from what He gave you, and He gave you the Holy Qur'an, in which:

وَلاَ رَطْبٍ وَلاَ يَابِسٍ إِلاَّ فِى كِتَابٍ مُّبِينٍ

(There is not) anything fresh or dry (green or withered) but is (inscribed) in a Clear Book.[24]

Both the living and the non-living are mentioned in this Book, but you have to extract it, you have to work! Every one of us is working for *dunyā* to get something in order to live. Okay, but for *Ākhirah* we need something to live on also, is it not? Allāh ﷻ is not telling you to stop working, but rather, "As you work for *dunyā,* work for *Ākhirah.* Be good!" That is what He is asking from you.

There are secrets in the Holy Qur'an. Just as when you go to your car and ignite the starter a spark comes and the car runs, there are secrets that you pass through in the Holy Qur'an by which Allāh ﷻ will ignite the light in your heart! Allāh ﷻ will ignite the forgiveness in your heart and He will order everyone who has permission to make *shafaʿah,* intercession on the Day of Judgment to intercede for you, especially *shafaʿat an-Nabī* ﷺ, the intercession of the Prophet ﷺ!

Holy Qur'an Written on the Forehead

When Allāh ﷻ ordered the angels to make *sajdatu 'l-iḥtirām,* prostration of respect to Sayyīdinā Adam ؑ—not *sajdatu 'l-ʿibadāh,* prostration of

---

[24] Sūratu 'l-Anʿam, 6:59.

worship, which is only for Allāh ﷻ—it was for the Light of Sayyīdinā Muḥammad ﷺ in the forehead of Sayyīdinā Adam ؑ. The first angel to make the prostration was Sayyīdinā Isrāfīl ؑ, who is the angel who will blow the Trumpet on the Day of Judgment. He was shaking to make that *sajda,* fearing Allāh ﷻ, in fear that he would not do it well, in fear of what would happen to him. For that reason, Allāh ﷻ wrote the entire Holy Qur'an in between his two eyes, on his forehead! That is Allāh's Greatness! Imam al-Qurṭubī said, "This (honor) was granted for that prostration of respect to the Light of Sayyīdinā Muḥammad ﷺ."

What do you think of the prostration of someone who is making *'ibādah* to Allāh ﷻ, making many prostrations every day? What will Allāh ﷻ give for the *sajda* of worship to Allāh ﷻ? He will give the Holy Qur'an written on your forehead and will give you much more! Every time you make a *sajda,* it will not be the same meaning that He expressed the first time He put the Holy Qur'an on your forehead; each time you make *sajda,* different meanings will come from these verses. They are the same verses, the same Qur'an that He put; the words are the same, but the meanings are different in every *sajda,* because your forehead is moving newly into *sajda* each time. *Allāhu Akbar*! So, if you make ten *sajdas* a day, you get ten different interpretations.

وَمَا يَعْلَمُ تَأْوِيلَهُ إِلاَّ اللهُ وَالرَّاسِخُونَ فِى الْعِلْمِ يَقُولُونَ آمَنَّا بِهِ كُلٌّ مِّنْ عِندِ رَبِّنَا وَمَا يَذَّكَّرُ إِلاَّ أُوْلُواْ الألْبَابِ

But none except God knows its final meaning. Therefore, those who are deeply rooted in knowledge say, "We believe in it; the whole (of the Divine Book) is from our Sustainer." And none will grasp the Message except Men of Understanding.[25]

No one knows these interpretations of the Holy Qur'an (*tā'wīl*) except Allāh ﷻ, and He will give them to you. He already passed it to the Prophet ﷺ: "The Sincere Pious Ones will say, 'We believed.'" It means, these interpretations are for the *Ummah*. There is no way we can define *Kalāmullāh*, the Words of Allāh ﷻ, as they are His Uncreated Words.

Allāh ﷻ created us and in our creation, we are limited in our understanding. Allāh's Understanding is not limited, and He gave that to the Prophet ﷺ, who is an ocean of knowledge!

What are these knowledges? As the *Awlīyāullāh* say, all knowledge that all prophets, all Companions of the Prophet ﷺ and all scholars took is only a drop from the Knowledge Ocean of

[25] Sūrat Āli 'Imrān, 3:7.

Prophet Muḥammad ﷺ. All of them are swimming in a single drop!

So where can academicians come in? All academicians in this whole world, with all that they have studied and written, took only a drop of that drop. That drop of the *Awlīyā* and *Ṣaḥābah,* who took from the Prophet Muḥammad ﷺ, became an ocean, relatively speaking, compared to the knowledge of academicians.

All of Holy Qur'an Is *Dhikr*

The Holy Qur'an is Divine; it is Allāh's Uncreated Words. So, when someone mentions Allāh's Words, will Allāh ﷻ be happy with him or not? Allāh ﷻ will say, "*ʿAbdī yadhkurunī,* My Servant is remembering Me!"

In what manner are you remembering Allāh ﷻ? The simplest way to remember is by reading the Holy Qur'an. You read or recite the Holy Qur'an, which contains power of Heavens, but also there is the power of reading the holy letters of the Holy Qur'an. For example, if you say the letter "*Alif* (ا)" in "*Alif. Lām. Mīm.* (الم)," Allāh ﷻ will say, "*ʿAbdī dhakaranī,* My Servant is remembering Me." If you say "*Lām* (ل)," Allāh ﷻ will say, "*ʿAbdī dhakaranī,* My Servant is remembering Me!" And if you say "*Mīm* (م)," Allāh ﷻ will say, "*ʿAbdī dhakaranī,* My Servant is remembering Me!"

Allāh ﷻ expresses His Name as "Allāh (الله)," so the letter *Alif* (ا) expresses the Greatness of Allāh ﷻ, as it is standing alone, which represents Oneness. *Lām* (ل) expresses two kingdoms, both *Mulk,* the Worldly Kingdom and *Malakūt,* the Heavenly Kingdom, while *Mīm* (م) represents Sayyīdinā Muḥammad ﷺ. So, when you say "*Mīm,*" Allāh ﷻ says, "*ʿAbdī dhakaranī wa ṣalla ʿalā nabīyyī,* My Servant is remembering Me and praising My Prophet!" and He sends ten *Ṣalawāt* on you!

Allāh ﷻ gave a secret to every verse and every letter in the Holy Qur'an. Take any word, for example: "*Dhālika* (ذلك)" from the verse "*Dhālika 'l-kitāb* (ذلك الْكتاب), that Book":

الٓمٓ ذَٰلِكَ الْكِتَابُ لَا رَيْبَ فِيهِ هُدًى لِّلْمُتَّقِينَ

> *Alif. Lām. Mīm. That is the Book about which there is no doubt, a Guidance for those conscious of Allāh.*[26]

If you say the letter "*Dhā* (ذ)," Allāh says "'*Abdī dhakaranī,* My Servant remembered Me." Even though it is normal Arabic, but because it is in the Holy Qur'an, it became Divine and is considered a Holy Name of Allāh ﷻ! Although it has no meaning without the continuation of the verse, when you say "*Dhā* (ذ)," Allāh ﷻ says, "'*Abdī*

[26] Sūratu 'l-Baqarah, 2:1-2.

dhakaranī, My Servant remembered Me," and when you say the letter *"Lām* (ل)," Allāh says, "*ʿAbdī dhakaranī,*" and when you say the letter "*Kāf* (ك)," once again, Allāh says "*ʿAbdī dhakaranī.*"

فَاذْكُرُونِى أَذْكُرْكُمْ وَاشْكُرُوا لِى وَلاَ تَكْفُرُونِ

Remember Me, I will remember you. Give thanks to Me and do not be ungrateful towards Me.[27]

So, since the word "*Dhālika*" is Divine, you can make *Dhikr* of it! Similarly, the word "*Muttaqīn* (متقين), those conscious of Allāh," can also be a *Dhikr*. Allāh ﷻ said, "For sure, this Book, there is no doubt in it, and it is Guidance for the pious servants." This holy verse alone will dress you with piety, even if you aren't pious, and will make you pious as you read what Allāh ﷻ granted us.

"I am reading, '*Alif. Lām. Mīm.*' *Yā Rabbī!* '*Dhālika 'l-kitābu lā rayba fīhi hudan li 'l-muttaqīn,* there is no doubt in this Book that it is a Guidance for those with *taqwā*, piety,' and there is no doubt in anyone reading the Holy Qur'an!" That means, Allāh ﷻ already described you as "*Muttaqīn,*" meaning, a *Mu'min*, Believer; you do not have any doubts, as you are reading the Holy Qur'an with a full belief, so it becomes Guidance for you to be pious. Since you are reading that verse, you are dressed with

[27] Sūratu 'l-Baqarah, 2:152.

being of the *Muttaqīn,* which indicates Holy Qur'an is a Guidance for the pious.

When you are dressed in that dress, do you think Allāh ﷻ will take that dress away from you on the Day of Judgment? The quality of a generous person is that when he gives you a dress, the next time he sees you, he will give you a new dress. You give him a dress every time he comes to you, and that way they accumulate. You will not take it back later and say, "Give me back the dresses I gave you!" So, every dress you take from Allāh ﷻ will accumulate up to the Day of Judgment, not only up to the day you die, as the Qur'an is the Eternal, Living Words of Allāh ﷻ.

If you take a computer and press the keys to write "Allāh," or order it with your voice, the computer will continuously write or say, *"Allāh, Allāh, Allāh."* It will keep writing as long as it functions, saying, *"Allāh, Allāh, Allāh."* If that is for a computer, what do you think happens when you are reading the Holy Qur'an? Do you think these *āyāt,* verses, will not keep repeating? Any verse you recite will continue to read itself, by itself nonstop, for Eternity!

Heavenly *Dhikrullāh* is different from *dunyā Dhikr*; *Ākhirah Dhikr* is continuous! The Holy Qur'an is moving in one *khatm* by itself, by heavenly 'computers.' So, if you read it in one complete sitting, in one day every day, then Allāh ﷻ will make angels recite *khatm* on your behalf. If you do a *khatm* every month and you read one *juz* every day, then it is as if in every month one *khatm* is read by angels. If you read another *khatm*, then it will be repeated by angels the next month. *Dhikrullāh* is *Dhikrun Ḥayy*, Living Remembrance; it is not dormant like our *Dhikr*. It is a continuous, Living *Dhikr*.

So, every verse of Holy Qur'an is *Dhikrullāh*. And Allāh ﷻ said in a Holy *Ḥadīth*:

عَنِ الْحَسَنِ، قَالَ: قَالَ رَسُولُ اللَّهِ صَلَّى اللَّهُ عَلَيْهِ وَسَلَّمَ: يَقُولُ اللَّهُ تَعَالَى إِذَا كَانَ الْغَالِبُ عَلَى عَبْدِي الِاشْتِغَالُ بِي جَعَلْتُ نَعِيمَهُ وَلَذَّتَهُ فِي ذِكْرِي فَإِذَا جَعَلْتُ نَعِيمَهُ وَلَذَّتَهُ فِي ذِكْرِي عَشِقَنِي وَعَشِقْتُهُ، فَإِذَا عَشِقَنِي وَعَشِقْتُهُ رَفَعْتُ الْحِجَابَ فِيمَا بَيْنِي وَبَيْنَهُ وَصِرْتُ مَعَالِمًا بَيْنَ عَيْنَيْهِ وَلَا يَسْهُو إِذَا سهى النَّاسُ، أُولَئِكَ كَلَامُهُمْ كَلَامُ الْأَنْبِيَاءِ، أُولَئِكَ الْأَبْطَالُ حَقًّا، أُولَئِكَ الَّذِينَ إِذَا أَرَدْتُ بِأَهْلِ الْأَرْضِ عُقُوبَةً وَعَذَابًا ذَكَرْتُهُمْ فَصَرَفْتُ ذَلِكَ عَنْهُمْ

> *If My servant is overtaken by being busy with all his mind and heart in remembering Me, I will make his blessings and his pleasure in continuously remembering Me through his heart. And when he makes his blessings and his pleasure in continuously remembering Me through his heart he will yearn for Me and I will yearn for him. I will raise the veils that are between Myself and himself and he will become a learned one before Me, and he will not be overwhelmed with fear when all*

human beings are overwhelmed with fear. Such ones, their words are like the words of the prophets. Those ones are the true heroes. Those are the ones, whom if I want to punish the people of the earth or torture them, I remember their presence and for their sakes I ward that off from the people.[28]

That is why, *Awlīyāullāh* went through that road and found that *Dhikrullāh*, Divine Remembrance is important in our life. As Sayyīdinā 'Alī al-Khawwāṣ ق said, "There is no better honor for a person, and the only *karāmah*, miracle a person can be happy with is *Dhikrullāh*." Here "*Dhikrullāh*" means *Dhikr* of "*Lā ilāha illa 'Llah*" or "*Allāh*" or *Dhikr* coming from Holy Qur'an, as all these *Asmā*, Divine Names are coming from Holy Qur'an. Don't say, "*Dhikr* is only to make negation and affirmation (i.e. saying '*Lā ilāha illa 'Llah*, there is no god by Allāh')," but rather, *Dhikrullāh* is any "Living Words"! So, anything you read from the Holy Qur'an is considered *Dhikrullāh*:

إِنَّا نَحْنُ نَزَّلْنَا الذِّكْرَ وَإِنَّا لَهُ لَحَافِظُونَ

Indeed, it is We who sent down the Dhikr (the Qur'an) and indeed, We will be its Guardian.[29]

---

[28] Abū Naʿīm in his *Ḥilya*, from al-Ḥasan ☼.

[29] Sūratu 'l-Ḥijr, 15:9.

One *murīd*, disciple of Sayyīdinā ʿAlī al-Khawwās ق was ordered to make seclusion for one continuous year. It is not easy: when you go for only forty days, you begin to count the days, and the last week seems like more than forty days!

So, he was in seclusion for one year, making *Dhikrullāh*, and as soon as he felt a miracle, he would mention that to the shaykh, because in seclusion you have to report what happens to you to the shaykh every day, if he is near. If not, then you report to him spiritually, because the shaykh has to know what happened to you. So, he mentioned a particular miracle that happened to him on that day. He went to the shaykh and forgot he was still in seclusion, meaning, he was continuously in *Dhikrullāh*, which is a true miracle in every moment, but from which he was veiled.

The shaykh said, "You were in a major miracle, sitting (*jalīs*) in the Nearness of Allāh ﷻ for one year, not feeling that daily constant miracle, and now you are coming here to tell me you experienced a miracle that is minor?"

As Allāh ﷻ says:

أَنَا جَلِيْسُ مَنْ ذَكَرَنِى

Anā jalīsu man dhakaranī.
I sit with him who remembers Me.[30]

---

[30] Ahmad, Bayhaqi.

"Jalīs," means "sitting beside" (metaphorically). So, by *Dhikr*, remembering Allāh ﷻ, you become so near to the Divine Presence, as Sayyīdinā 'Alī Hujwirī ق said, *"Dhikrullāh* is one of the main pillars in the Way of Allāh ﷻ!"

So, don't drop reading the Holy Qur'an, and try to read at least one page daily!

الله

Reading of the Holy Qur’an

The Determination of the Believer

Aʿūdhu billāhi min ash-shayṭāni 'r-rajīm.

Bismillāhi 'r-Raḥmāni 'r-Raḥīm.

The verses in the Holy Qur'an are talking, living verses, and you will be dressed in endless rewards by reading them. So read, as rewards and blessings accumulate! However, Shayṭān doesn't want us to read, so he will give you hundreds of excuses to not read.

I usually read Qur'an in the mornings, but one morning, when I began to read, the telephone kept ringing. There were problems I had to figure out, which took three hours and made us to be late for *Ẓuhr* prayer. After *Ẓuhr*, I went back and thought, "*Alḥamdulillāh,* there is no disturbance at this time," and tried to read again, when another message came that required me to step in and solve it. It disturbs you day and night, so the best is to turn off your phone! Now, they have made people busy with these small handheld phones, and instead of taking time to read the Holy Qur'an, people fill their time with text messaging. Any time I begin to read the Holy Qur'an, the telephone rings and sometimes I unplug it, as that is the best way.

So Shayṭān doesn't let you enter a "Living Favor," because it is his field to keep you away. That is why it is said:

القُرَان هُو طَردُ الغَفْلَةُ بِأَى وَجْهٍ تَيَسَر

Al-Qur'ān hūwa ṭardu 'l-ghaflah, bi ayyi wajhin tayyassar.

"To read the Holy Qur'an is to throw away heedlessness from you."

SubḥānAllāh, these are old quotes from scholars who came hundreds of years ago. At that time, they didn't have translations of *Qur'ān* in Turkish, Urdu or other languages; it was only in Arabic and the only knowledge and education was Islamic—there was no other education. Everything focused on Islamic Jurisprudence (*Fiqh*), *Ḥadīth* or Holy Qur'an and its interpretation, nothing else. It is said, "There will come a time when the meanings of Holy Qur'an will be in many different languages so that other people may understand; it will come in any form for those Muslims who do not know Arabic." This was indicated hundreds of years ago, that you would be able to understand Holy Qur'an in different languages. Even reading it in that form will throw away heedlessness!

Importance of Reading from Multiple Copies of the Qur'an

Grandshaykh ʿAbdAllāh ق and Mawlānā Shaykh Nazim ق said, "If you have ten *masāḥif,* copies of the Holy Qur'an, after you complete a reading of the Qur'an, then start reading from a different copy, so as not to let them sit on the shelf and complain, *'Hajaranī ʿabdī,* my servant deserted me!'" If you have ten, read one, then another, then another, because they will all witness for you on the Day of Judgment.

Although they are all written the same, this practice shows respect to Allāh's Words, not to leave them on the shelf, forgetting about the Holy Qur'an. You may also give the copies as a gift and then get ten more, because the Holy Qur'an is living.

That is why in some written copies of the Qur'an, there is a supplication at the end, *Duʿā Khatmu 'l-Qur'an*, and for each letter of the alphabet there is a *duʿā* with the plea, "Let Holy Qur'an be with me in *dunyā* and in *Ākhirah,* and lead me to *Sirāṭa 'l-Musṭaqīm,* the Straight Path. Let it be a Light in the grave and discipline us with the character of the Holy Qur'an, as each of its words is a Beautiful Divine Name, *yā* Allāh!"

So, do not leave reading the Holy Qur'an! Whenever you have time, read it and don't be lazy by listening to Shayṭān, as we are lazy and struggling. We ask for Allāh's Forgiveness!

If You Cannot Read, Use Your Fingers!

If you don't know how to read, then do as many scholars and many *Awlīyāullāh* recommended, which is to pass your fingers under the verses and look at them, beginning from right to left. If you want to read the meaning in English, no problem, but pass your fingers under the Arabic, because there are lights coming from these letters that will enter directly into your heart.

Every letter in the Holy Qur'an contains an immense power that Allāh ﷻ gave the people who use the Arabic language. Grandshaykh ق said, "The *Shahādah* finger is connected to the heart. So, as you are reading the Holy Qur'an by passing your finger under the Holy Words, light comes into the heart and will be a witness for you on the Day of Judgment!"

Also, in order to learn more, you can check *ma'anī al-Qur'an,* the meanings of the Holy Qur'an, as converts are unable to understand the original Arabic. May Allāh ﷻ guide us to understand the meanings of the verses of Holy Qur'an in order that it will intercede for us on the Day of Judgment! And indeed the Holy Qur'an will intercede for everyone who reads it.

Don't underestimate the power of the Holy Qur'an; every letter is more powerful than the light of the sun! You see the sun? There are 70,000 suns like our sun! Our sun is fifty-million degrees centigrade. The second sun is not going to be fifty-million degrees centigrade, but it is doubled and the third is tripled and the fourth is quadrupled; each one's power is more intense than the first one. So, the letters of the Holy Qur'an are like suns coming to dress you when you are reading!

Where are we from understanding the Holy Qur'an? Yet with all its immense greatness, Allāh ﷻ is still telling us to read the Qur'an, so read it.

وَرَتِّلِ الْقُرْآنَ تَرْتِيلاً

Recite the Qur'an in slow, measured rhythmic tones.[31]

Some Companions of the Prophet ﷺ used to make one *khatm*, completing the whole Qur'an every day! It takes about twelve or fifteen hours. How long does it take with you? Twenty minutes per *juz,* and thirty *juz* is around sixteen hours. When they were free, they were reciting, but why should they be free? They were in battles while their tongues were reciting! Not like us. We can make one hundred *Ṣalawāt,* salutations on the Prophet ﷺ, for example, and get tired, and Allāh ﷻ is

[31] Sūratu 'l-Muzzamil, 73:4.

saying to make nonstop *Ṣalawāt*. If Allāh ﷻ did not love us, He would not tell us to make *Ṣalawāt*.

The Angels of Answering

Grandshaykh 'AbdAllāh al-Fa'iz ad-Daghestani ق said that even if someone makes seven mistakes in reciting *al-Fātiḥa,* the angels will correct it, and Allāh ﷻ knows best. Allāh ﷻ has created a special kind of angels. You cannot count them, as they are infinite in number; no one knows their number except their Creator. Their praising, their *Dhikr* is by only one word that Allāh ﷻ gave them to say. He gave them a specific name, the Angels of Answering.

Allāh ﷻ said to the Prophet ﷺ:

> (O Muḥammad!) I gave you something that I did not give any prophets before you, which no other prophet could carry. Even before I decided to give you the Holy Qur'an, My Ancient Holy Words, I created these special angels for Holy Qur'an. When the Qur'an comes to you and you reveal it to people who then read it, these angels will come and repeat "*Āmīn*!" after every letter. As soon as the person opens the Qur'an and says "Alif," the angels will say "*Āmīn*!" If you say "*Āmīn,*" they will say "*Āmīn.*" If you say "*Dhālika 'l-kitābu lā rayba fīh...,*" they will say, "*Āmīn, āmīn, āmīn...*" On every letter of the Holy

> Qur'an, I have created different angels for the different people who are reading—in every moment a new angel is created whose only job is to say "*Āmīn*!" causing that reciter to be dipped into that letter's ocean of knowledge.

Allāh ﷻ opens the knowledge for the heart of that servant without his knowing. For instance, if someone reads *Sūratu 'l-Fātiḥa*, then for every letter Allāh ﷻ opens an ocean of knowledge.[32] From one person to another, the meaning changes and with the meaning also changes the light and knowledge of each letter in the Holy Qur'an. Each ocean of knowledge that appears from the letters of the Holy Qur'an alters the oceans of knowledge that appeared from the previous letters.

The light from each letter that the angels say "*Āmīn*" for will appear for the person on the Day of Judgment. If a person is trying his best to read the Holy Qur'an and makes nine mistakes out of 10, with only one word correct, then Allāh ﷻ sends these angels and makes them to recite the Qur'an correctly so that He can disburse the rewards given to the servant who reads it correctly—thus, He rewards the servant and opens that knowledge to his or her heart! Allāh ﷻ sends

---

[32] *Sūratu 'l-Fātiḥa* comprises 139 letters, including "*Bismillāhi 'r-Raḥmāni 'r-Raḥīm*" at the beginning.

them, and they descend on every person who recites the Holy Qur'an from beginning to end.

The Descension of 72,000 Angels

When someone completes the Holy Qur'an from beginning to end, Allāh ﷻ sends 72,000 angels. When that servant finishes reading, Allāh ﷻ will accept his supplication, even if he made mistakes in his recitation, as these 72,000 angels correct the mistakes and say, "*Āmīn*!" That is why they are called the Angels of Answering. Even if he makes nine mistakes out of ten, Allāh ﷻ sends those 72,000 angels to correct them. It is very important to make supplication at the end of the Qur'an, because Allāh ﷻ has sent His Holy Book to His Beloved Prophet ﷺ to make His Prophet ﷺ great. The greatness of the Holy Qur'an is shown when these angels come to make supplication!

Grandshaykh ق says that the bodies of these angels are soft and subtle, not like ours. Allāh ﷻ makes His Angels great. Their forms are so subtle that 700,000 can stand in the place of a finger and yet there is room for all of them to stand there. Allāh ﷻ makes them very tall on the Day of Judgement, like the *muadhdhin*, the one who calls to prayer. They say "*Āmīn*!" higher than any person does on Judgment Day. From their height, they have a vista of fifty years journey. With that height they are saying "*Āmīn*!" and giving responses for the person who is reciting.

Gaining the Reward of Reading the Whole Qur'an

عَن رَجَاء الغَنَوِى قَالَ: قَالَ: رَسُولُ الله ﷺ: " مَن قَرَأَ قُلْ هُوَ اللهُ أَحَدٌ ثَلَاثَ مِرَارٍ فَكَأَنَّمَا قَرَأَ القُرآن أجمَع "

That is why, to make it easy for people, the Prophet ﷺ said, *"Whoever reads Sūratu 'l-Ikhlāṣ, the Chapter of Sincerity three times, it is as if he has read the whole entire Qur'an!"*[33]

So, what are we waiting for? Read it three times:

أَعوذُ بِاللهِ مِنَ الشَّيْطانِ الرَّجيم

بِسْمِ اللهِ الرَّحْمٰنِ الرَّحِيمِ

قُلْ هُوَ اللَّهُ أَحَدٌ ﴿١﴾ اللَّهُ الصَّمَدُ ﴿٢﴾ لَمْ يَلِدْ وَلَمْ يُولَدْ ﴿٣﴾ وَلَمْ يَكُنْ لَهُ كُفُوًا أَحَدٌ ﴿٤﴾

A'ūdhu billāhi min ash-shayṭāni 'r-rajīm

Bismillāhi 'r-Raḥmāni 'r-Raḥīm.

Qul Hūw Allāhu Āḥad, Allāhu' ṣ-Ṣamad, lam yalid wa lam yūlad wa lam yaku 'l-lahū kufūwan āḥad.

---

33 Al-'Aqīlī, from Rajā al-Ghinawī. *Saḥīḥ Bukhārī*, Abū Sa'īd al-Khuḍrī.

I seek refuge in Allāh from the accursed Shayṭān.

In the Name of Allāh, Most Gracious, Most Merciful. Say, "He is the One God, God the Eternal, the Uncaused Cause of All Being. He begets not nor is He begotten and there is nothing that could be compared to Him."[34]

Every one of us just made *Khatm al-Qur'an*! And when you read it in *jama'ah,* a gathering, you get the benefit of reading in a gathering, which means it is multiplied.

O Muslims and Believers! May Allāh ﷻ put in our heart the value of Holy Qur'an. I am not saying I am better than you or you are better than me, but we are all in the same ditch and we want to come out.

إنّمَا الأَعْمَالُ بِالنّيّاتِ،

As the Prophet ﷺ said in a *Ḥadīth ash-Sharīf*:

Every action is according to its intention (nīyyah).[35]

So, make your *nīyyah* and move, *inshā-Allāh*!

❁

[34] Sūratu 'l-Ikhlāṣ, 112:1-4.

[35] Bukhārī and Muslim.

Mystery Letters of the Holy Qur'an

Al-Ḥurūf al-Muqaṭṭaʿāt

Aʿūdhu billāhi min ash-shayṭāni 'r-rajīm.

Bismillāhi 'r-Raḥmāni 'r-Raḥīm.

As we have said, no one can completely understand the Holy Qur'an. *Awlīyāullāh* are pulling out and extracting meanings from each verse. Not only the *āyāt*, verses of Holy Qur'an, but there are *aḥruf*, letters that are at the beginning of some *sūrahs* called, *"al-Muqaṭṭaʿāt,"* abbreviations. Every letter is an ocean, and the knowledge in these letters cannot be limited; they are from pre-Existence, as they are Allāh's Words, which has no beginning and no end.

Do not think the Holy Qur'an is only what they translate to you in the commentary. Every letter in the Holy Qur'an is a Letter of Light coming from the Holy Divine Name, *an-Nūr.* So, every letter in the Holy Qur'an has a meaning, which we can only know through a word, but there are fourteen special letter combinations in the Holy Qur'an that are not words but are full of secrets known as *"al- Muqaṭṭaʿāt."*

Alif. Lām. Mīm.

One of these special letter combinations is *"Alif. Lām. Mīm.* (الم)"? What is the significance of these letters? *"Alif. Lām. Mīm."* is the first *Muqaṭṭaʿāt* in the Holy Qur'an. In Arabic, we call them *aḥruf*, letters. We don't know their meaning, but if Allāh ﷻ opens, He gives *Awlīyāullāh* meaning.

Alif (ا) symbolizes and guides you towards Allāh ﷻ, because it is the first letter of His Beautiful Name and the first letter of the Arabic alphabet. *Alif* is Allāh's Absolute Existence, *al-Wujūd al-muṭlaq lillāhi taʿālā*, no one else's; we don't exist, as we are going to go, but Allāh ﷻ is the Creator. When He orders the angel Isrāfīl عليه السلام to blow on the Trumpet, every living and non-living thing will melt, disappear; no one will be left, not even the angels.

Allāh ﷻ says in the Holy Qur'an:

لِّمَنِ الْمُلْكُ الْيَوْمَ لِلَّهِ الْوَاحِدِ الْقَهَّارِ

> *Whose will be the Dominion that Day? That of Allāh, The One, The Irresistible!*[36]

Allāh ﷻ is answering Himself by Himself. He ﷻ is saying, "To whom is the Kingdom today, O Kings, O Presidents, O Ministers, O Muslims, O Believers, O Unbelievers, all those who consider themselves something! O Shaykhs, O *Awlīyāullāh*,

---

[36] Sūratu 'l-Mu'min, 40:16.

O Prophets?" There will be no one on Earth anymore. He orders the Earth cleaned and says to Himself by Himself, "*Lillāhi 'l-Wāḥidi 'l-Qahhār*! *Al-Mulk*, The Dominion, is for Allāh ﷻ, *Al-Qahhār*, The Subduer, The Overpowering, He is The One Who has everything in His Hand!" This is only a little bit of explanation of the letter *Alif*.

If you take away the *Alif* from "Allāh (الله)," the word becomes "*lillāh* (لله)." The meaning changes completely, from The Absolute Existence, Allāh, to *lillāh*, which means, "Everything is for Him." If you take away the first *Lām*, you will be left with "*Lahu* (له), to Him," and if you remove the second *Lām*, it will become "*Hu* (ه)": *Qul Hūw Allāhu Āḥad*, "Say to them, *yā* Muḥammad, that there is no existence for anyone! *Qul Hūwa*, say, 'He is The Unknown One; no one can see Him, as He is The Creator and The Hidden Treasure.'" (112:1)

As Allāh ﷻ says in a Holy *Ḥadīth*:

كُنْتُ كَنْزا مَخْفِيًا فَأَحْبَبْتُ أَن أُعْرَف فَخَلَقْتُ الخَلْق وَبِهِ عَرَفُونِى

I was a Hidden Treasure (and) I wanted to be known, so I created Creation, and through that they knew Me.[37]

---

[37] Cited by al-Alūsī in *Rūḥ al-Maʿanī* with variant renditions from al-Samhūdī and as-Sakhāwi, none of which can be attributed to the Prophet ﷺ.

Allāh ﷻ said, *"Qul Hūw Allāhu Āḥad. Yā* Muḥammad! Say *'Hū,'* The Hidden Treasure, that no one knows about." So, His Essence, His Reality is hidden through the letter *Hā* (ه).

Where are all the meanings of these four letters in "Allāh (الله)" hidden? In the *muqqata'āt, "Alif. Lām. Mīm.* (الم)".

The *Lām* (ل) represents the angel Jibrīl ﷺ, because directly after the Beautiful Name of Allāh ﷻ, represented by *Alif* in *"Alif. Lām. Mīm."* comes *Lām,* which is the letter facing the Divine Presence. Who was facing the Divine Presence waiting for orders and for the Revelation to be given to him, to send to all the prophets, messengers and to Sayyīdinā Muḥammad ﷺ? It was Jibrīl ﷺ. So, that *Lām* represents him, and we are not going to go too much further.

Then, we come to the last one, which is *Mīm* (م). How many *Mīms* are there in the letter *Mīm* when the letter itself is spelled out? There are two *Mīms* (ميم): one is *mutaḥarrik,* accented while the other is *sākin,* silent. The meaning is hidden between these two *Mīms,* which is the letter *Yā* (ى). In Arabic grammar, the *Yā* is *Alif,* so between the two *Mīms* there is an *Alif,* the first letter of the Name "Allāh".

So, one *Mīm* is facing Jibrīl ﷺ, facing Allāh ﷻ, and the other *Mīm* is facing the *Ummah*, the Nation of Muḥammad ﷺ. The first *Mīm* is focusing on the Divine Presence, while the second *Mīm* is what the Prophet ﷺ took of Revelation from Jibrīl ؑ that no one knows about except himself and Allāh ﷻ, Who revealed it to him. The *Mīm* that comes facing the *Ummah* is a drop of an ocean, as the Prophet ﷺ reduced it in order for people to carry it, giving according to our capacity:

لَا يُكَلِّفُ ٱللَّهُ نَفْسًا إِلَّا وُسْعَهَا ۚ لَهَا مَا كَسَبَتْ وَعَلَيْهَا مَا ٱكْتَسَبَتْ

> *On no soul does Allāh place a burden greater than it can bear.*[38]

If the Prophet ﷺ expressed the Revelation exactly as revealed to Him, then people could not carry it, as it belongs to Prophet Muḥammad ﷺ.

So, in between these two *mīms* is an ocean of knowledge, *'Ulūmu 'l-Awwalīn wa 'l-Akhirīn*, Knowledge of Before and After, because the *Yā* (ى) is *Alif* (ا). The first *Mīm* receives and the second *Mīm* gives, because when they take, they have to give; they don't keep to themselves.

Whatever is hidden is in between the two *Mīms*. When *Awlīyāullāh* want to look at their followers, they look from the two *Mīms* in order to see what they are doing, from what the Prophet ﷺ gave them from a little bit of drops of Reality, as it is an ocean, and they are able to dive in that.

---

[38] Sūratu 'l-Baqarah, 2:286.

Awlīyāullāh know the relationship they have built with Prophet ﷺ, and whatever they take they have to give out. *Awlīyāullāh,* Mawlānā Shaykh Nazim ق and Mawlānā Shaykh ʿAbdAllāh al-Daghestani ق, built up the reality of the *Ṭarīqah,* as there are too many secrets and it is impossible to express them, as people might not understand.

Kāf. Hā. Yā. ʿAyn. Ṣād.

When Allāh ﷻ opens for the *Ummah* as He opened for the Companions of the Prophet ﷺ, they become Light upon Light! We are weak servants and Allāh ﷻ will raise us when we love His Beloved One, Sayyīdinā Muḥammad ﷺ as His *ʿAbd,* and Allāh ﷻ revealed the Holy Qur'an on His Prophet ﷺ.

What do you have to say to begin reading *Sūrat Maryam*? "*Kāf. Hā. Yā. ʿAyn. Ṣād.* (كهيعص)," which is another one of these *al- Muqaṭṭaʿāt.*

When Jibrīl ؑ came to the Prophet ﷺ and said, "*Kāf,*" the Prophet ﷺ said, "'*Alimtu,* I knew." Jibrīl ؑ was shocked. From where did he know? "I'm revealing you the Message just now." How did he know? He knew it and he knew all interpretations and meanings that Allāh ﷻ wanted him to know!

Where are scholars? There were many previous scholars who wrote books on these acronyms. Today, where are scholars like that? With all that, it is nothing and still in limits.

Then Jibrīl ﷺ said, "*Hā,*" and again the Prophet ﷺ said, "'*Alimtu,* I knew." Today, when you ask a scholar, "What is '*Kāf. Hā. Yā. 'Ayn. Ṣād?*'" he will say, "I don't know, Allāh knows," which is correct. Can anyone give a commentary on it? No way.

I heard Grandshaykh 'AbdAllāh, may Allāh bless his soul, say that when Jibrīl ﷺ said, "*Kāf*" and the Prophet ﷺ said, "'*Alimtu,*" it means whichever words begin with the letter "*Kāf*" in the Arabic dictionary, the knowledge of their secrets immediately came to the Prophet ﷺ, and not from the dictionary made by human beings, but from the Heavenly dictionary!

How many words begin with the letter *Kāf* in both the Heavenly and worldly interpretations? Normally, it might be eight hundred to one thousand.

Alif is mentioned 2,800 times. So, when Jibrīl ﷺ said, "*Kāf,*" the Prophet ﷺ said, "I know." When he said, "*Hā,*" the Prophet ﷺ said, "'*Alimtu,* I know it already!" "*Yā,*" "I know!" "'*Ayn,*" "I know!" "*Ṣād,*" "I know!"

Jibrīl ﷺ was finished, he could say no more as he was stuck. What was there to say? That means the Prophet ﷺ has received the interpretations through a revelation directly to his heart, as the Prophet ﷺ once said, "I have been taught the Knowledge of Before and the Knowledge of After, *'Ulūm al-Awwalīn wa 'l-Akhirīn.*"

So why does *Sūrah Maryam* begin with "*Kāf* (ك)"? *Kun fayakūn*, "'Be!' and it will be." (36:82) The first letter of Creation is "*Kāf*" in "*Kun* (كُنْ), Be!" and Allāh's Order is between the "*Kāf* (ك)" and the "*Nūn* (ن)." So when Jibrīl ﷺ said, "*Kāf*," what the Prophet ﷺ knew we don't know. Whatever Allāh ﷻ gave the Prophet ﷺ from His Love to him, the Prophet ﷺ will give to the *Ummah*. There are people who will understand whatever the Prophet ﷺ sent to them.

What Allāh ﷻ said in the Holy Qur'an, "*Alif. Lām. Mīm*" and "*Kāf. Hā. Yā. ʿAyn. Ṣād,*" all have meanings. *ʿUlamā* say they have an infinite number of meanings on these *Muqaṭṭaʿāt*, and all of these meanings have been given to the Prophet ﷺ, because he represents *Ismu 'Llāh al-ʿAẓam*, the Greatest Name of Allāh ﷻ! As Sayyīdinā Abū Ḥanīfa said, "*Ismu 'Llāh al-ʿAẓam* is The Name Allāh." When Sayyīdinā Mūsā ﷺ asked to see Allāh ﷻ, he wanted to know *Ismu 'Llāh al-ʿAẓam*, because with it you can do anything, *kun fayakūn*,

إِنَّمَا أَمْرُهُ إِذَا أَرَادَ شَيْئًا أَنْ يَقُولَ لَهُ كُنْ فَيَكُونُ

But His command, when He intends a thing, is only that He says to it: "Be! and it is."[39]

But no, it was only given to the Prophet ﷺ!

---

[39] Sūrah Yāsīn, 36:82.

عن سعيد بن جبير قال هى أسماء الله تعالى (مقطعة) لو علم الناس تأليفها لعلموا اسم الله الأعظم .

As the *Tabiʿ* Saʿīd ibn Jubayr said,

> The (*al-Muqaṭṭaʿāt*) are Names from the Holy Divine Names of Allāh ﷻ. If people knew their composition, they would know Allah's Greatest Name.[40]

May Allāh grant us forgiveness for the sake of His Beautiful Name, *Ismu 'Llāh al-ʿAẓam.*

[40] Reported by Īmām Baghāwī in his *Tafsīr*.

الله

The Expression of Majesty, "Allah!"

Calling on Allāh ﷻ by His Name

Aʿūdhu billāhi min ash-shayṭāni 'r-rajīm.

Bismillāhi 'r-Raḥmāni 'r-Raḥīm.

Kalimat at-Tawḥīd, the Word of Oneness, to say, *"Lā ilāha illa 'Llāh Muḥammadun Rasūlullāh,"* cleans the *kufr* (disbelief) and *shirk* (polytheism) from the servant; you are purified by it and it benefits you. Allāh ﷻ is happy that we are agreeing and accepting *Kalimat at-Tawḥīd*, but if you call Him by His Name, "Allāh," He will be even more happy with you! We might say, *"Lā ilāha illa 'Llāh Muḥammadun Rasūlullāh,"* but when you say, "Allāh," it is different.

Kalimat at-Tawḥīd is like a trademark you must have on everything, but *Lafẓ al-Jalāla*, the Expression of Majesty, to call on Allāh ﷻ directly, is very difficult. It means, you have moved forward from *Maqām at-Tawḥīd*, the Station of Oneness to *Maqām al-Āḥadiyya*, the Station of Uniqueness; you have moved from everything you can see in front of you that indicates The Creator to the Station of Uniqueness, where there is only One, the Divine Presence. Just by calling on His Name, they will take you from *Maqām at-*

Tawḥīd to the Divine Presence, *Ṣāḥib al-Mulki wa'l-Malakūt*.

Decorate Your Hearts with "Allāh!"

Alḥamdulillah that Allāh ﷻ put *Lafẓ al-Jalāla*, His Majestic Name on our tongues. I am happy with some copies of the Holy Qur'an, as they praise Allāh ﷻ and express their feelings by coloring the Holy Name of Allāh ﷻ. Wherever the Name "Allāh" is mentioned, you see it in red; they decorate the Name in red, so it stands out. *Zayyanū qulūbakum min Qur'ān aw zayyina masājidakum bi 'l-Qur'ān*, "Decorate your hearts or your mosques with the Holy Qur'an." It will stay there, as Allāh ﷻ will give it a color by His Angels; He will order the angels to go to the reciters of Qur'an and give them a Heavenly color for that!

Some people wrongly say, "Don't do *Dhikr* by the tongue, it is *ḥarām, shirk, bid'a, kufr*!" So, if it is *ḥarām* to make *Dhikr* of "Allāh," why aren't they saying for these highlighted *masāḥif* to be thrown away? For them, why isn't that *ḥarām, shirk, bid'a, kufr?* They don't want us to say "Allāh," but Allāh ﷻ Himself says, "*Qul Allāh*, say 'Allāh!'"

قُلِ الله ثُمَّ ذَرْهُمْ فِى خَوْضِهِمْ يَلْعَبُونَ

> *Say "Allāh!" then leave them to plunge in vain discourse and trifling.*[41]

When you say "Allāh," that is enough, you don't need anything else. He told us in the verse to say, "Allāh," so we say, "Allāh!" Leave the others to play with their *dunyā* matters. When you say "Allāh," Allāh ﷻ responds, as He mentioned to His Prophet ﷺ in this Holy *Ḥadīth*:

عَنْ أَبِى هُرَيْرَةَ رَضِىَ اللَّهُ عَنْهُ قَالَ: قَالَ النَّبِىُّ صَلَّى اللَّهُ عَلَيْهِ وَسَلَّمَ : "يَقُولُ اللَّهُ تَعَالَى: أَنَا عِنْدَ ظَنِّ عَبْدِى بِى، وَأَنَا مَعَهُ إِذَا ذَكَرَنِى، فَإِنْ ذَكَرَنِى فِى نَفْسِهِ، ذَكَرْتُهُ فِى نَفْسِى، وَإِنْ ذَكَرَنِى فِى مَلَإٍ، ذَكَرْتُهُ فِى مَلَإٍ خَيْرٍ مِنْهُمْ، وَإِنْ تَقَرَّبَ إِلَىَّ بِشِبْرٍ، تَقَرَّبْتُ إِلَيْهِ ذِرَاعًا، وَإِنْ تَقَرَّبَ إِلَىَّ ذِرَاعًا، تَقَرَّبْتُ إِلَيْهِ بَاعًا(١) وَإِنْ أَتَانِى يَمْشِى، أَتَيْتُهُ هَرْوَلَةً" (رواه البخارى وكذلك مسلم والترمذى وابن ماجه)

> *I am as My Servant thinks of Me, and I am with him when he remembers Me. If he remembers Me to himself, then I remember him to Myself. If He remembers Me in a group, then I remember him in a group better than it. Whoever approaches Me by a hand's span, I approach him by an arm's length. Whoever approaches Me by an arm's length, I*

---

[41] Sūratu 'l-An'am, 6:91.

approach him by two arm's length. If he comes to Me walking, I come to him running.[42]

That is *Dhikrullāh*. You can recite as much *Ṣalawāt* as you can, because it goes to your heart easily, but whenever you sit to make *Dhikrullāh* of "*Allāh, Allāh, Allāh, Allāh, Allāh,*" it becomes heavy and you stop, as it is carrying a lot. You cannot carry what Allāh ﷻ gives you when you say the *Ism al-Jalāla,* as we haven't yet reached tranquility in our hearts:

أَلَا بِذِكْرِ اللهِ تَطْمَئِنُّ الْقُلُوبُ

Truly in the remembrance of Allāh do hearts find tranquility.[43]

The Lady Saint Whose Heart Found Tranquility

There was a very well-known *Walī* and *ʿAlīm* from Baghdad, Ḥasan al-Baṣrī ق. One time, as he was leaving the city to go back home, he saw Rābiʿah al-ʿAdawīyya ق sitting in the desert and was astonished to see both wild and domestic animals gathering around her in peace. It was a circle of love where no one touched the other, all sitting

[42] Bukhārī, Muslim, Tirmidhī, Ibn Majah.

[43] Sūrat ar-Raʿd, 13:28.

quietly and listening as she made her *Dhikr* of *"Allāh, Allāh, Allāh, Allāh...!"*

All the animals sat around her listening, but as soon as Sayyīdinā Ḥasan al-Baṣrī ق approached, they all ran away, because it was not in his heart; he had not yet reached her level.

Rābiʿah al-ʿAdawīyya ق had accumulated power through reading *Lafz al-Jalāla,* the Expression of Majesty, *"Allāh, Allāh, Allāh,"* that satisfied her after she carried a very heavy load for seven years. She ق said, "It took me seven years to make *Dhikrullāh* with the intention that I destroy what is blocking me from *Lafz al-Jalāla.*" She spent seven years doing *Dhikr* of "*Allāh, Allāh.*" Her ego told her, "No, it is too much, don't do it." She said, "No, I will continue to overcome all obstacles until I reach the reality of *Dhikrullāh*!" She said, "And Allāh opened it for me." She was asking, "*Yā Rabbī*! I want the *Nūr,* Light of Your Name, *Lafẓ al-Jalāla,* to come to my heart. Even if it is as small as the eye of a needle, it will be enough for me."

Whenever you sit down to make *Dhikr* of "Allāh," with or without *tasbīḥ,* immediately you begin to feel heavy and you stop. Or, Shayṭān comes in many different ways: as a human gossiping in your ear, on the phone, an alarm clock ringing, or you begin to feel sleepy. All this will come to you in order to distract you from that *Dhikr,* and it took her seven years to eliminate these obstacles!

The more you recite *Lafẓ al-Jalāla*, "Allāh," one after another, the more it begins to come on your tongue easily.

So, after those seven years, whenever she sat to make *Dhikr* of *Lafẓ al-Jalāla,* she felt peace and happiness; she was satisfied with *Dhikrullāh* as her heart was connected with the Divine Presence. She felt tranquility and ease, like when some people swim, they float on their backs. This means, the density of the body is balanced, like with wood and iron: iron cannot float, but wood can. *Allāhu Akbar*! Our body cannot float, but our soul can. *Ṭu'mānīna,* tranquility pulls the body up and makes it float. That is why people can float, because they surrender to the ocean, they don't feel afraid; if you feel even a little afraid, you sink. *Iṭmi'nān* is when you have peace and ease: Allāh ﷻ creates love in your heart from *Lafẓ al-Jalāla* and you are dressed with that in order to come to Him clean and pure.

So, she developed tranquility in her heart by which she surrendered completely and did not feel heavy, which is why she was floating. Her student, Ḥasan al-Baṣrī ق hadn't reached that level yet: he was drowning and that's why the animals ran away, and he knew he needed to perfect his heart with *Dhikrullāh*.

The Light of *Ism al-Jalāla* can change everything in you and rejuvenate you! That is why they call it

Ism al-Jalāla, Ismu 'Llāh al-ʿAẓam, the Greatest Name of Allāh's Ninety-Nine Names, which is "Allāh."

الله

Sulṭān adh-Dhikr

The *Dhikr* that Penetrates Heavens and Earth

A'ūdhu billāhi min ash-shayṭāni 'r-rajīm.

Bismillāhi 'r-Raḥmāni 'r-Raḥīm.

يَا مَعْشَرَ الْجِنِّ وَالْإِنسِ إِنِ اسْتَطَعْتُمْ أَن تَنفُذُوا مِنْ أَقْطَارِ السَّمَاوَاتِ
وَالْأَرْضِ فَانفُذُوا لَا تَنفُذُونَ إِلَّا بِسُلْطَانٍ

> *O you assembly of jinns and men! If you can pass beyond the zones of the Heavens and the earth, pass. Not without authority (a Sulṭān) shall you be able to pass.*[44]

Allāh ﷻ is saying, "If you are able to penetrate from the atmosphere of the earth, then do it, but you cannot do it without a *Sulṭān*," which is *Sulṭān adh-Dhikr*. *Sulṭān adh-Dhikr* is of two levels: one is to mention Allāh by the Name that encompasses all His Beautiful Names and Attributes, "Allāh," which is the highest *Dhikr* that has no higher equivalent, and the other is the Holy Qur'an,

---

[44] Sūratu 'r-Raḥmān, 55:3.

which is Allāh's Ancient Words and His Highest Knowledge.

Sulṭān adh-Dhikr means "The Highest Heavenly Book in Allāh's Ancient Words," which is the Holy Qur'an, and that is the *Sulṭān* that takes you to penetrate the earth's atmosphere.

إِنَّا نَحْنُ نَزَّلْنَا الذِّكْرَ وَإِنَّا لَهُ لَحَافِظُونَ

> *Behold! It is We Ourselves Who have bestowed from on High, step by step, this Reminder (Dhikr) and behold, it is We Who shall truly guard it.*[45]

"Al-Dhikr" here means the Holy Qur'an, and Allāh ﷻ is The One protecting it. That's why there is no better book. Holy Qur'an is Allāh's Words which are alive: when you read Holy Qur'an, Allāh's Words rejuvenate you from everything negative.

The *Khatm al-Qur'an* of *Awlīyāullāh*

Some *Awlīyā* get the power to read *Sulṭān adh-Dhikr* through the Holy Qur'an. There are *Awlīyā* who complete Holy Qur'an in one month; they read one *juz* every day, while others read it in one week or one day!

---

[45] Sūratu 'l-Ḥijr, 15:9.

There are *Awlīyā* who read the Holy Qur'an including the interpretation, not only the literal meaning, but *tā'wīl:*

وَمَا يَعْلَمُ تَأْوِيلَهُ إِلاَّ اللهُ وَالرَّاسِخُونَ فِى الْعِلْمِ يَقُولُونَ آمَنَّا بِهِ كُلٌّ مِّنْ عِندِ رَبِّنَا

> *No one knows the interpretation of the Holy Qur'an except Allāh, and those who are firmly grounded in knowledge say, "We believe in the Book; the whole of it is from our Lord."*[46]

That is the knowledge that Allāh ﷻ embedded in every *sūrah*. So, *Sulṭān adh-Dhikr* is to recite the Holy Qur'an and extract the meaning; it might take you one year or ten years. Some *Awlīyā* were not able to achieve it in all their life, so they get it in the grave. How long does it take you? *Awlīyā* compare among themselves how many times they accomplished the *Sulṭān adh-Dhikr*, the *khatm* of Holy Qur'an with interpretation. Some accomplished it twice in their lives, some ten, some one hundred, and some did it every moment in their lives.

Grandshaykh 'AbdAllāh ق and Mawlānā Shaykh Nazim ق, may Allāh bless their souls, said that there are nine *Awlīyāullāh* in the Naqshbandi Sufi Order that have read the Qur'an with *Sulṭān adh-*

---

[46] Sūrat Āli 'Imrān, 3:7.

Dhikr, the highest way of remembering Allāh ﷻ and His Prophet ﷺ.

Awlīyāullāh also have one higher level of understanding what *Sulṭān adh-Dhikr* is, and only nine *Awlīyā* knew that, which is to recite the Holy Qur'an with all its secrets!

After the *Ṣaḥābah* ؓ and the Family of the Prophet ﷺ, Sayyīdinā Abū Yazīd al-Bistāmī ق was the first one to recite the Qur'an once with *Sulṭān adh-Dhikr*, with all its secrets, which took him his whole life, because Grandshaykh ق said, "On every letter, Allāh ﷻ will open 24,000 oceans of knowledge." There are around 350,000 letters in the Holy Qur'an. Multiply 24,000 by 350,000 and that is the number of oceans of knowledge that opened to Sayyīdinā Abū Yazīd al-Bistāmī ق, and each one receives different oceans of knowledge, all of which comes from the Divine Presence with the *barakah* of Sayyīdinā Muḥammad ﷺ and our Grandshaykhs! So Sayyīdinā Bayāzīd was able to do it once, and other *Awlīyāullāh* did it three, five and seven times.

Grandshaykh's ق *Khatm* with Every Breath

Grandshaykh ق mentioned that Allāh ﷻ gave Shaykh Sharafuddin ق the power, through the Prophet ﷺ, to complete *Sulṭān adh-Dhikr* with every inhale and exhale, completing the Holy Qur'an with all its secrets! With that out-breath come different secrets than on the in-breath. And in reality, Grandshaykh was talking about himself.

That is what we have been mentioning about *an-nafas aṭ-ṭāhir,* when you mention Allāh's Name, Allāh ﷻ creates an angel from that breath that will make *tasbīḥ* on your behalf and it will ask Allāh ﷻ to have mercy on you because you mentioned Allāh's Name, *Lafẓat al-Jalāla. Qul Allāh,* "Say 'Allāh!'" Allāh ﷻ will create an angel to mention Him and it will be written for you.

So, there are *Awlīyā* who, when they read the Holy Qur'an, they read with interpretation according to the power that Allāh ﷻ gave to them. They are not like us.

Shaykh Sharafuddin ق was making *Khatm al-Qur'an* on every breath in and out! That is *Ṭayyu 'l-Lisān,* to fold the tongue, and that is how Allāh ﷻ gave *'Ulūmu 'l-Awwalīn wa 'l-Akhirīn* to the Prophet ﷺ in *kun fayakun,* "Be! And it will be." In less than a second, before The Pen had even started to write.

May Allāh ﷻ grant us that *Sulṭān adh-Dhikr*: with every breath in and every breath out to be *Khatm al-Qur'an:*

وَمَا ذَٰلِكَ عَلَى اللَّهِ بِعَزِيزٍ

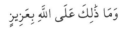

And that is not difficult for Allāh.[47]

If you think, "Allāh will give me that," you will get it! If you doubt it, then Allāh ﷻ says to His Angels, "Leave him alone until he has no doubt in his heart!"

وَقَالُواْ سَمِعْنَا وَأَطَعْنَا غُفْرَانَكَ رَبَّنَا وَإِلَيْكَ الْمَصِيرُ

And they say, 'We hear, and we obey. (We seek) Your forgiveness, our Lord, and to You is the end of all journeys.[48]

So, we say, "*Āmannā wa ṣadaqnā, samiʿnā wa ataʿanā*!, We believe and confirm what You said, Our Lord, we hear and we obey!"

[47] Sūrat Ibrāhīm, 14:20.

[48] Sūratu 'l-Baqarah, 2:28.

Coming of Imam Mahdī

Khāmis al-Qur'an, Secrets of the Qur'an

A'ūdhu billāhi min ash-shayṭāni 'r-rajīm.

Bismillāhi 'r-Raḥmāni 'r-Raḥīm.

So, the secrets that all prophets wanted Allāh to give them to use are embedded in the first verses of every chapter in the Holy Qur'an, but Allāh only gave them to Sayyīdinā Muḥammad and He will keep it until Sayyīdinā al-Mahdī comes. When Mahdī comes, then the interpretation of the Holy Qur'an will be opened. *InshāAllāh,* the salvation and opening is coming! Sayyīdinā Mahdī is coming! Search for him.

All these knowledges, *'Ulūm al-Awwalīn wa 'l-Ākhirīn,* Knowledge of Before and After, will come and be distributed to the *Ummah* according to their levels. It will not be given in books, as all these books are going to disappear.

Today, when they print books, they use ink. What is in ink? Urea. They use the chemicals of urine so the printing will be strong, and the ink will stay. That will not be allowed in the time of al-Mahdī; only pure ones will be allowed, and only pure manuscripts will remain.

In the time of Imam al-Mahdī ﷺ you won't need to read a book and go through studying, as knowledge will be given through the reflection of eyes from one to another. It will go from the one who received the knowledge to your eyes and to your heart. Then, you will reflect to another, he to another, and so on.

So, all this is going to go and only *Khāmis al-Qur'an,* which is the Secret of Holy Qur'an will remain, nothing else. At that time, people will follow *Khāmis al-Qur'an,* the knowledge of extracting all secrets embedded in every *sūrah, ayah* and letter!

Grandshaykh, may Allāh bless his soul, used to say there are 24,000 Oceans of Knowledge on every letter of the Holy Qur'an, which Allāh ﷻ will open to *Awlīyāullāh*. That is what we need, and the Prophet ﷺ already gave that to Sayyīdinā 'Alī ؓ.

،"أنَا مَدِينَةُ الْعِلمَ وَعَلِيٌ بَابُهَا"

As the Prophet ﷺ said:

I am the City of Knowledge and 'Alī is its Door.[49]

He gave Sayyīdinā 'Alī ؓ the door, so he is responsible for who can enter, but everyone will go in, as Allāh's Mercy is wide and because we are

---

[49] Al-Ḥākim in his *Mustadrak*.

all children of Sayyīdinā Muḥammad ﷺ, some through blood, some through spirituality.

As-salāmu ʿalayka yā Sayyīdī, yā Rasūlullāh, yā Raḥmatan li 'l-ʿālamīn!

Qur'anic Openings to the Greatest Divine Name

Aʿūdhu billāhi min ash-shayṭāni 'r-rajīm.

Bismillāhi 'r-Raḥmāni 'r-Raḥīm.

Shaykh Hisham Kabbani's son, Dr. Nour Kabbani reciting the first verses of each chapter in the Holy Qur'an from his father's handwritten notebook. Ramadan 2018.

Grandshaykh ʿAbdAllāh ad-Daghestani, may Allāh bless his soul, said that *Ismu 'Llāh al-ʿAẓam*, Allāh's Greatest Name, has been given to *Awlīyāullāh* from the Prophet ﷺ *fī awāili 's-sūwar*, in the beginning of every *sūrah* in the Holy Qur'an, from *Sūratu 'l-Fātiḥa* all the way to *Sūratu 'n-Nās*.

That is why he ق gave me his notebook, handwritten in very beautiful calligraphy by his shaykh, Shaykh Sharafuddin ad-Daghestani ق that I copied by hand, as there were no copying machines at that time. It contains *awā'ili 's-sūwar,* the first verses of each *sūrah,* which is what we recite in *Tarāwīḥ* prayer. If you begin reciting from beginning to end, in one of these *sūrahs* you will pass through The All-Encompassing Name, *Ismu 'Llāh al-ʿAẓam,* but you don't know which one it is. That's why it is recommended to read these verses.

We can write it and pass it to people. Sometimes it is one verse and sometimes it is two, depending on the *sūrah,* and that has been given to the Prophet ﷺ!

Daily *Wird* of *Awlīyāullāh*

Ismu 'Llāh al-ʿAẓam derives from the Name "Allāh," *Lafẓ al-Jalāla,* but the Name itself we don't know: it is hidden, embedded in one of the first verses of the 114 chapters in the Holy Qur'an. *As* Sayyīdinā Abū Bakr aṣ-Ṣiddīq ؓ said:

لله فی کل کتاب مِن کُتُبه سر، وسِرُّه فی القرآن أوائل السور .

Allāh has in every Book a secret, and His secret in the Quran is in the openings of the sūras.[50]

---

[50] This is also reported from the other three Khulafā ar-Rāshidūn and ibn Masʿūd, may Allah be pleased with them,

So, if you read the first three verses of every *sūrah,* for sure you will have read *Ismu 'Llāh al-ʿAẓam,* and it will be written for you as if you knew *Ismu 'Llāh al-ʿAẓam.* Even if you do it once in your lifetime, it is accepted. *Awlīyāullāh* made it their daily *wird* to recite the first three *ayahs* from every *sūrah*!

We are weak, *yā Rabbī*! This advice is for all of us, for the *Ummah* and anyone listening. We are more in need of the advice as they are better than us; at least they are listening from far away, while we sat together, I can see you and you can see me, but they are following without being here. May Allāh ﷻ bless all who are listening. *Allāhu Akbar!*

---

as reported by Abū Layth as-Samarqandī in his *Tafsīr* and Īmām Baghāwī in his *Tafsīr*.

الله

Allāh's Greatest Name

The Request of All Previous Prophets

Allāh ﷻ manifests Himself to all prophets through His Beautiful Names and Attributes. Allāh ﷻ gave every prophet a way to carry and dress in a different Name of His Beautiful Names, and Prophet Muḥammad ﷺ is the one that is *Khātim al-Anbīyā,* the Seal of Messengers. Allāh ﷻ is manifesting Himself on him ﷺ through *Ismu 'dh-Dhāt,* the Name that encompasses all Beautiful Names and Attributes, which is "Allāh." That carries a lot of knowledge to the Prophet ﷺ, and under it come all the different Beautiful Names and Attributes.

"Allāh" represents the Name of Allāh's Essence, which no one can know: *Qul Hūwa Allāh, "Say, 'The One Who is Unknown is Allāh."*[51] If you say "Allāh" it means "Allāh, the Creator," and He is known through His Beautiful Names and Attributes.

Every prophet asked for the secret of *Ismu 'Llāh al-'Aẓam,* but Allāh ﷻ only gave it to Sayyīdinā Muḥammad ﷺ. Sayyīdinā Mūsā عليه السلام asked for it and

---

[51] Sūratu 'l-Ikhlāṣ, 112:1.

Allāh ﷻ didn't give it to him, which is why he asked:

قَالَ رَبِّ أَرِنِى أَنظُرْ إِلَيْكَ قَالَ لَن تَرَانِى وَلَـكِنِ انظُرْ إِلَى الْجَبَلِ فَإِنِ اسْتَقَرَّ مَكَانَهُ فَسَوْفَ تَرَانِى

> *"O my Lord! Show Yourself to me that I may look upon You." Allāh said, "By no means can you see Me (directly), but look upon the mountain: if it abides in its place, then you shall see Me."*[52]

He said, "*Yā* Allāh, let me see you." Allāh ﷻ said, "No, you cannot see Me. If you want to see Me, look upon the mountain and I will send My Manifestation (*Tajallī*). If it stays the way it is, then you can see Me. If it shatters, then you cannot."

فَلَمَّا تَجَلَّى رَبُّهُ لِلْجَبَلِ جَعَلَهُ دَكًّا وَخَرَّ موسَى صَعِقًا

> *When his Lord manifested His Glory on the mount, He made it as dust and Moses fainted.*[53]

When Allāh ﷻ manifested His Beautiful Name "Allāh" on the mountain, it completely shattered to dust. Mūsā ﷺ fainted as if he had an electric shock, like hospitals use to restore a patient's heartbeat.

---

[52] Sūratu 'l-Aʿrāf, 7:143.

[53] Sūratu 'l-Aʿrāf, 7:143.

We are asking Allāh ﷻ to give us that power in order to open all our hearts. All prophets asked for *Ismu 'Llāh al-ʿAẓam,* but Allāh ﷻ didn't reveal it. The Prophet ﷺ went to the Divine Presence with the secret of *Ismu 'Llāh al-ʿAẓam,* not because Sayyīdinā Jibrīl ﵇ was accompanying him, but because Allāh ﷻ wanted him to be dressed from that Reality, so that he may know the Greatness of his Creator and that he ﷺ is His Servant.

Wa min Allāhi 't-tawfīq, bi ḥurmati 'l-Fātiḥa.

الله

The Secret of Allāh's Greatest Name

Bismillāhi 'r-Raḥmāni 'r-Raḥīm. Allāhumma ṣalli wa sallim ʿalā Sayyīdinā Muḥammad wa ʿalā āli Sayyīdinā Muḥammad.

When we make *duʿā,* we say *taḥmīd, "Alḥamdulillāh rabbi 'l ʿalamīn wa 'ṣ-ṣalātu wa 's-salāmu ʿalayka ayyuha 'n-nabī...,"* then we continue the *duʿā,* but most important:

عن النبى صلى الله عليه وسلم: "لايرد دعاءٌ أوله بسم الله الرحمن الرحيم ..."

> *The Prophet ﷺ said, "Duʿā is never rejected when it begins with "Bismillāhi 'r-Raḥmāni 'r-Raḥīm."*[54]

Why? Because it contains three of Allāh's Precious Names, which they say are the "Beautiful Names," to demonstrate there is no beauty in this universe or Heavens without Allāh's Beautiful Names and Attributes. Allāh's Names make everything beautiful! When Allāh ﷻ created the Pen, He ordered it to write *Lā ilāha ill 'Llāh Muḥammadun Rasūlullāh,* "There is no creator except Allāh and Muḥammad is His Messenger."

---

[54] Al-Zamakhsharī in his *tafsīr Rabīʿ al-Abrār.*

So whatever the Prophet ﷺ says is real, *lā shak wa lā shubha,* without objection or doubt.

3,000 Divine Names in Heavenly Revealed Books

Mawlānā Shaykh Nazim ق once said:

> There are a total of 3,000 Names of Allāh Almighty: 1,000 for the angels; 1,000 for the prophets; 300 in the Torah; 300 in the Bible; 300 in the Psalms; and 99 in the Holy Qur'an, altogether making 2,999, and there is one *Ismu 'Llāh al-ʿAẓam,* Allāh's Greatest Name. Allāh Almighty made these 3,000 Names into three Names and presented them to Sayyīdinā Muḥammad ﷺ and his Nation, which is "*Bismillāhi 'r-Raḥmāni 'r-Raḥīm*"! So, if a person says, "*Bismillāhi 'r-Raḥmāni 'r-Raḥīm,*" he is actually saying the 3,000 Holy Names of our Lord, including the Greatest One! The keys of miracles are with "*Bismillāhi 'r-Raḥmāni 'r-Raḥīm*!

Who among the *Ṣaḥābah* ؓ ever had doubt about what the Prophet ﷺ said? Anything the Prophet ﷺ said, Sayyīdinā Abū Bakr aṣ-Ṣiddīq ؓ said, "*Ṣadaqta, yā Rasūlullāh.*" The Message came to a people who were unaware of Islam, so when it came, some principles were too much for them, like the story of the *Miʿrāj*. On his return, the Prophet ﷺ stood on a hill and said, "Last night I

went for *Isrā' wa 'l-Mi'rāj*." '*Isrā*" means that *sarā
fi 'l-layl,* he moved at night across this world.

Hearing this news, the *Ṣaḥābah* ✿ vacillated
between acceptance and denial, but Sayyīdinā
Abū Bakr aṣ-Ṣiddīq ✿ immediately said, "*Ṣadaqta
yā Rasūlullāh*! Yes, what you said is the truth,"
because Sayyīdinā Muḥammad ﷺ and Sayyīdinā
Abū Bakr aṣ-Ṣiddīq ✿ shared a mutual love. So
when the Prophet ﷺ approached *Qāba Qawsayni
aw Adnā* he was not afraid, but he felt the
loneliness of the situation and wanted familiarity
to feel okay. So Allāh made him hear the
movement and feel the presence of Sayyīdinā Abū
Bakr aṣ-Ṣiddīq ✿; then he became *aṭma'ana
Rasūlullāh, muṭma'in,* tranquil, because he sensed
a friend was with him.

That is why when someone dies he is worried and
feels *khashyā,* fear of Allāh, fear of what is going to
happen, as he is alone and has no family with him.
That is why some people say to leave the light on
in the room he is in, as his soul comes back to the
house where he died to get *uns,* familiarity. That
is why the Prophet ﷺ said, "I will be shoulder-to-
shoulder in the grave with the *mu'min* who
remembered me in *dunyā* to give him a feeling of
familiarity." That is because when Prophet ﷺ was
in *Qāba Qawsayni aw Adnā,* the Station of Two
Bows' lengths or Nearer, Allāh ﷻ made him hear
the sound of Sayyīdinā Abū Bakr aṣ-Ṣiddīq ✿ and
then he relaxed, which is how he knew Prophet ﷺ

was in the *Mi'rāj*. So upon hearing the announcement he quickly said, "*Ṣadaqta yā Rasūlullāh*! Yes, what you said is the truth!"

Sayyīdinā 'Umar ☙ received knowledge and advice from both Sayyīdinā Abū Bakr aṣ-Ṣiddīq ☙ and Sayyīdinā 'Alī ☙ and it is well known that were it not for Sayyīdinā 'Alī ☙, Sayyīdinā 'Umar ☙ would have made two mistakes in his decisions. So, whatever you do in your life you must say, "*Bismillāhi 'r-Raḥmāni 'r-Raḥīm*" as *Ismullāh al-'Aẓam* is in it. If anyone truly knows what *Ismullāh al-'Aẓam* is, he can say, "*Kun! Fayakūn*" and that will come into existence!

When Allāh created Creation, He dressed them with the Reality of *Ismullāh al-'Aẓam*. Whom did He dress? Prophet ☙ was the first to be created, so Allāh dressed the Light of the Prophet ☙ with the Reality of *Ismullāh al-'Aẓam*. So when you look at the Prophet ☙ you see the Light of *Ismullāh al-'Aẓam,* and for that reason he didn't shatter when the Qur'an was revealed to him; *Ismullāh al-'Aẓam* is in the Qur'an, so he was able to carry it.

The Vision of Allah ☙ in Paradise

Grandshaykh `Abd Allah ق said, and I quote here from his notes:

> According to the hadith, Prophet ☙ said that every *mu'min* in the highest level of Paradise will see Allāh ☙. What Prophet ☙ meant by

> this was also in accordance with what we know, that nothing can contain Allāh. So how can we see Him? Allāh ﷻ dresses the Prophet ﷺ, *al-Insān al-Kāmil,* with 3,000 of Allāh's Beautiful Names and Attributes, and afterwards manifests His Greatest Name on him, *Ismullāh al-ʿAẓam,* dressing the Prophet ﷺ with that Light. People see it and feel they saw Allāh ﷻ, although that is impossible because Allāh cannot be seen; even the Prophet ﷺ, who reached *Qāba Qawsayni aw Adnā*—Two Bows' Length or Nearer the Divine Presence—still cannot see The Essence. He can see manifestations of Allāh's Beautiful Names and Attributes, but He cannot see the Reality of The Essence. He can see what emanates from The Essence, manifestations of not only those 3,000 Beautiful Names, but all of them!

We already explained the 3,000 Beautiful Names and Attributes that ﷻ Allāh made known: 1,000 to His Angels, 1,000 to His Prophets, 300 are in the *Zabūr,* 300 in the *Injīl,* 300 in the *Tawrāt,* and ninety-nine in the Holy Qur'an, and all these Names are in the Qur'an. The ninety-nine Beautiful Names and Attributes are the heart of these 3,000 Names, and *Ismullāh al-ʿAẓam* is the heart of the ninety-nine Beautiful Names and Attributes.

So the Light of *Ismullāh al-ʿAẓam* will manifest on the Prophet ﷺ and shine on that Paradise, and through the Perfect One, Sayyīdinā Muḥammad ﷺ, those Lights will appear and who is in that Paradise will see it on him and think it is Allāh Himself! Allāh lets them feel He is appearing, but actually His Light appears because no one can carry His Original Appearance, which is from *al-Nūr*, from which everything comes into light. If there is no light in this room you could not see anything here, but when there is *nūr* you can see everything.

Grandshaykh ق continues:

> Then Allāh ﷻ orders the Prophet ﷺ to send the *mu'mins* who are in this Paradise to go one after another to different levels of Paradise carrying that *Nūr*. They are dressed with the Light of *Ismullāh al-ʿAẓam* from the Light that is dressed on the Prophet ﷺ, and when they appear, the people of that Paradise think they are seeing Allāh ﷻ, while in reality it is the *mu'min* who appears from the Paradise of *Muḥammadīyyūn*, shining with that Light the Prophet ﷺ dressed them with:

ما وسعنى أرضى ولا سمائى ولكن وسعنى قلب عبدى المؤمن

Neither My Heavens nor My Earth contain Me, but the heart of My Believing Servant contains Me.[55]

There is no way that anything can contain Allāh ﷻ, but that Light settled in the heart of Abū Bakr aṣ-Ṣiddīq ؓ and that's why he is different from everyone else and favored the most, because that Light comes from that secret in his heart that he was carrying from Prophet ﷺ.

مَا فَضَلَ أَبُو بَكرِ النَّاسَ بِكَثْرَةُ صَلاةٍ وَلَا بِكَثْرَةُ صِيَامٍ، وَلَكِن بِشَيءٍ وَقَرَ فِي قَلْبِه،

Abū Bakr does not surpass you because of fasting or praying more, but because of a secret that took root in his heart.[56]

Prophet ﷺ sent traces of the *Ismullāh al-ʿAẓam* to Sayyīdinā Abū Bakr aṣ-Ṣiddīq ؓ and Sayyīdinā ʿAlī ؓ.

---

[55] Hadith *Qudsī*, related in *al-Iḥyā* of Īmām al-Ghazālī.

[56] The description of Sayyidina Abū Bakr aṣ-Ṣiddīq ؓ by the Successor Bakr ʿAbdAllāh al-Maznī, related by al-Ḥakīm at-Tirmidhī, but often related as a hadith.

I am the City of Knowledge and ʿAlī is its Door (or Gate).[57]

Sayyīdinā ʿAlī ﷺ was at the door, but didn't enter inside because that is reserved for Sayyīdinā Abū Bakr aṣ-Ṣiddīq ﷺ; however, you cannot go inside without Sayyīdinā ʿAlī ﷺ. These three Names, "*ar-Raḥmān,*" "*ar-Raḥīm*" and "Allāh" are the Names Allāh likes best. They are from *ad-Dhāt,* the Essence, and they are not *Ṣiffāt,* Attributes, but they are not describing the Attributes. "*Ar-Raḥmān*" that is from His Mercy that He gives everyone what they want, both the *mu'min* and non-*mu'min*. "*Al-Karīm,*" the Generous One, will not take back any gift He gave, just as a *mu'min* does not take back any gift he gave. So under that *Ṣiffat ar-Raḥmah,* the Attribute of Mercy, Allāh gives.

Allāh ﷻ said:

الرَّحْمَنُ عَلَّمَ الْقُرْآنَ

Ar-Raḥmān ʿallam al-Qur'ān.

The Most Merciful has imparted this Qur'an.[58]

He didn't say, "*Allāh ar-Raḥmān ʿallam al-Qur'ān.*" He created many Names that describe that "*Ism ar-Raḥmān.*"

---

[57] al-Ḥākim, Tirmidhī.

[58] Sūrat ar-Raḥmān, 55:1,2.

عن أبى هريرة -رضى الله عنه- قال: سمعت رسول الله -صلى الله عليه وسلم- يقول: " جَعَلَ اللهُ الرحمةَ مائة جُزْءٍ، فَأَمْسَكَ عِنْدَهُ تِسْعَةً وَتِسْعِينَ، وأَنْزَلَ فى الأَرْضِ جُزْءًا وَاحِدًا، "

The Prophet ﷺ said Allāh ﷻ has divided Mercy into one-hundred parts: ninety-nine He kept with Himself and He sent to this earth one part from them...[59]

Allāh ﷻ gave through the Prophet one of these ninety-nine mercies to all *Āhlu 'd-dunyā'*, the inhabitants of this world. *Āhlu 'd-dunyā'* not only includes human beings, but also *jinn* and all created beings in this universe. From *Ismu 'r-Raḥmān,* The Divine Name, the Merciful, Allāh created one-hundred Names to describe that One Divine Name, and *dunyā* is under only one of them. Allāh provides for *Āhlu 'd-dunyā,* and He left ninety-nine Names of Mercy other than the ninety-nine Beautiful Names and Attributes for *Ākhira,* the Hereafter.

عَنْ أَبِى هُرَيْرَةَ رَضِىَ اللَّهُ عَنْهُ أَنَّ رَسُولَ اللَّهِ صَلَّى اللَّهُ عَلَيْهِ وَسَلَّمَ قَالَ: "إِنَّ لِلَّهِ تِسْعَةً وَتِسْعِينَ اسْمًا مِائَةً إِلا وَاحِدًا مَنْ أَحْصَاهَا دَخَلَ الْجَنَّةَ."

About these Names the Prophet ﷺ said:

---

[59] Bukhārī and Muslim from Abū Hurairah ؓ.

> *Allah has ninety-nine Names and whoever preserves them will enter Paradise.*[60]

Everyone is under these ninety-nine Names of Mercy, by which Allāh ﷻ is providing us whatever we are getting in *dunyā*: life, breath, cures, food....

The Immense Power of the Divine Attribute of Mercy

Why did He keep the other ninety-nine Names of *raḥmah*? Why didn't He send them to *dunyā*? Because everyone would faint from all of them! This whole *dunyā* got all that is here from one of them and we cannot carry more than that. Why did Allāh order us to make *ṣalawāt* on the Prophet ﷺ? Why did Allāh say, "I am making *ṣalawāt* and all My Angels are making *ṣalawāt*. So, O you Believers, make *ṣalawāt*!" Allāh ﷻ did that to create a cause for Him to give His Mercy, so He is sending *raḥmah* with His *Ṣalawāt* to raise the Prophet ﷺ higher and higher!

When we make *ṣalawāt*, Allāh ﷻ increases us with what He increases the Prophet ﷺ, which we explained in the series, *Salawat of Tremendous Blessings* (2012), at the beginning of Ramadan. For example, *Ṣalawāt al-Fātiḥ* is one line only, and when Muḥammad al-Talmaysānī ؓ completed reading *Dalā'il al-Khayrāt* 100,000 times, the

---

[60] Muslim.

Prophet ﷺ appeared to him in a dream saying, "O Muḥammad al-Talmaysānī! If you recite Ṣalawāt al-Fātiḥ, it will be as if you recited Dalā'il al-Khayrāt 800,000 times!" So if you recite this ṣalawāt three times before you sleep, it will be as if you recited Dalā'il al-Khayrāt 2,400,000 times!

So Allāh ﷻ will dress Sayyīdinā Muḥammad ﷺ with the ninety-nine Names of Raḥmah. That is why there must be traces of Ismullāh al-'Aẓam in these three Names, "Allāh," "ar-Raḥmān" and "ar-Raḥīm," which is why the Prophet ﷺ ordered us to recite "Bismillāhi 'r-Raḥmāni 'r-Raḥīm" with Surat al-Fātiḥah. That is equal to reciting the entire Holy Qur'an, as is reading "Qul Hūwa Allāhu Āḥad" three times.

Previously, Allāh did not allow any understanding of Ismullāh al-'Aẓam, as there was no one able to understand that, but in the no-time zone when Allāh created the Prophet ﷺ, in 'Alam ar-Rawḥanīyāt, the World of Meanings, Allāh introduced him to Bismillāhi 'r-Raḥmāni 'r-Raḥīm. Allāh didn't reveal that Greatest Name to Sayyīdinā Mūsā ؏ nor to any other Prophet, but when the Prophet ﷺ came to this dunyā from the World of Images, Allāh dressed him with the Light of His Beautiful Names and Attributes, Ismullāh al-'Aẓam, which only the Prophet ﷺ knows and which Awlīyāullāh can detect, but in a minimal way.

This knowledge is not in books, but rather it is in Grandshaykh's and Mawlana Shaykh Nazim's hearts, and they give information. Grandshaykh ق was like a fountain whenever he opened these subjects and it is impossible to quote everything he said.

The Most Merciful bestows His Favors and gives Creation from His Generosity; it means, He will appoint for His Creation what they need and remove afflictions from them. '*Ar-Raḥīm*' is if you ask Allāh accepts and if you don't ask from Him, He gets upset. Allāh likes to give to His Servant, so when you ask, He gives!

ادْعُونِى أَسْتَجِبْ لَكُمْ

Supplicate Me and I will give you![61]

If you don't ask He gets angry, because He takes that *ṣiffat* out of you, that is His Anger:

وَمَا نُرْسِلُ بِالآيَاتِ إِلاَّ تَخْوِيفًا

We never send Our Signs except to cause people to fear. [62]

"We don't send the verses of punishment except to make people fear!" So when you read verses of punishment, Allāh takes that punishment away

[61] Sūratu 'l-Mu'min, 40:60.

[62] Sūratu 'l-Isrā', 17:59.

from you, if you possess those characteristics that would cause you to be punished like that. And when you recite Holy Qur'an, those verses will take this all away and Allāh will dress you from His Holy Paradise. Therefore, Allāh likes His Servants to ask from Him! If you don't get what you ask for in this life, you will get it in the Next Life.

If you ask He will give, and if you don't ask He gets angry. To the contrary, if you ask human beings, they get angry! But Allāh likes to give, so ask Him, "*Yā Rabbī*! We are asking through Your Generosity to grant that we be with the Prophet ﷺ in *dunyā*, in death, in the grave, on Resurrection, during the Account." If you don't ask from Allāh ﷻ, He gets upset, so it is better to ask Him.

Who knew about these three Beautiful Names and Attributes, "Allāh," "*ar-Raḥmān*" and "*ar-Raḥīm*," and what descriptions they contain? What we are describing here is only to give a very limited understanding, not in a professional way, as *Awlīyāullāh* are not professionals. So, if you recite "*Bismillāhi 'r-Raḥmāni 'r-Raḥīm*," it is as if you mentioned Allāh ﷻ with all His Beautiful Names and Attributes! Also, whoever recites them will be dressed with all these 3,000 Beautiful Names and Attributes as if he made *dhikr* with them and knew all the infinite number of Allāh's Beautiful Names and Attributes! That will be dressed on you if you recite "*Bismillāhi 'r-Raḥmāni 'r-Raḥīm*" even once.

Four *Mīms*, Four Rivers

It is related in reports and in the *Sīrah* that Prophet ﷺ said, "On the night of *Isrā' wa 'l-Miʿrāj,* Allāh made me see all Paradises." He did not say "Seven Paradises;" he did not limit them, which means there are more than seven. Also, even Paradises cannot carry who will describe them and who will enter them. There are special Paradises and Allāh willing, Allāh will put us there. So, when Prophet ﷺ saw these Paradises, he saw four flowing rivers: one was a river of crystal water condensed from the water's coolness, a river of milk, then a river of wine and a river of honey.

According to Grandshaykh's notes, Prophet ﷺ said, "*Yā* Jibrīl! From where these rivers come and to where are they going?"

Sayyīdinā Jibrīl ؑ replied, "All these rivers come from the highest Paradise and then the ninety-nine Paradises unite and blend in that ocean."

What is that ocean Jibrīl ؑ is mentioning? The Prophet ﷺ was waiting for the answer, which is only for us to learn, as Prophet ﷺ already knew. That ocean is *Multaqā 'l-Baḥrayn,* the confluence of those four rivers, known as *Ḥawḍ al-Kawthar,* about which Allāh ﷻ said:

إِنَّا أَعْطَيْنَاكَ الْكَوْثَرَ

Innā aʿtaynāka 'l-kawthar.

> *Indeed, We have granted you, (O Muhammad), al-Kawthar.*[63]

Where they meet is a beautiful blending of water, milk, honey, and wine, which we have never tasted! *Inshā-Allāh* we will taste it in Paradise!

Prophet ﷺ said, "*Yā* Jibrīl! From where does it come?"

Sayyīdinā Jibrīl ﵇ said, "I don't know from where it comes, except that it comes from these four places. O Muḥammad! Ask Allāh to teach you from where these rivers come."

So, the Prophet ﷺ immediately asked, for otherwise Allāh would have been upset. As soon as he asked, an angel responsible for all those rivers came, greeted Prophet ﷺ and said, "Close your eyes, *yā* Muḥammad," and then, "Open your eyes."

Prophet explained, "I opened my eyes and saw a tree and a dome made of pearl, *Qubbat al-Arzāq*, the Dome of Provisions.

The root of the Arabic word for water, "*mā'*," is the letter *mīm*. So, the wine is coming from the *mīm* of *ar-Raḥmān* and honey is coming from the *mīm* of *ar- Raḥīm*, and from this knowledge Prophet ﷺ said, "Then I knew these four rivers come from someone who says '*Bismillāhi 'r-*

---

[63] Sūratu 'l-Kawthar, 108:1.

Raḥmāni 'r-Raḥīm.'" So, say *"Bismillāhi 'r-Raḥmāni 'r-Raḥīm!" Inshaa-Allāh,* may Allāh ﷻ make us drink from these four rivers!

Also, Allāh ﷻ said, "O Muḥammad! Whoever, mentioned Me by saying *'Bismillāhi 'r-Raḥmāni 'r-Raḥīm,'* without any desire of being seen, I will make him drink from these four rivers and his *du'ā* will never be rejected if it begins with *'Bismillāhi 'r-Raḥmāni 'r-Raḥīm.'*

O Allāh! For the sake of *Bismillāhi 'r-Raḥmāni 'r-Raḥīm,* forgive us and accept from us Ramadan on the last day, and take away from us all difficulties in health or wealth.

May Allāh ﷻ forgive us and may Allāh ﷻ bless us.

Wa min Allāhi 't-tawfiq, bi ḥurmati 'l-ḥabīb, bi ḥurmati 'l-Fātiḥa.

And with Allāh comes all success. For the sake of the Beloved we recite the opening chapter of Holy Qur'an.

الله

The First Verses of the Holy Qur'an

Shaykh Hisham Kabbani reciting the Holy Qur'an, beginning from the Opening Chapter, *Sūratu 'l-Fātiḥa.*

Aʿūdhu billāhi min ash-shayṭāni 'r-rajīm

Bismillāhi 'r-Raḥmāni 'r-Raḥīm.

I seek refuge in Allāh from the accursed Shayṭān.

In the Name of Allāh, Most Gracious, Most Merciful.

First, we are saying, "*Aʿūdhu billāhi min ash-shayṭāni 'r-rajīm.*" The order is in the Holy Qur'an to ask protection from Iblīs before reading Qur'an and before any matter, because Shayṭān is the root of all evil; without him there would be no evil. He is the biggest *fitna* for human beings, and he is their greatest, most dangerous enemy. May Allāh ﷻ disgrace him!

Don't think you are able to defeat Iblīs; he has thousands of tricks. May Allāh protect us from his evil and curse him. *Āmīn*. Ask for protection from Allāh ﷻ, as that is a weapon against Iblīs. When you read the Holy Qur'an, Shayṭān is focused on you, to prevent you from reading, but what about in other matters? Shayṭān never leaves you!

Therefore, we are saying, *"Aʿūdhu billāhi min ash-shayṭāni 'r-rajīm!"*

سُورَةُ الْفَاتِحَةِ

1) Sūratu 'l-Fātiḥa
The Opening

بِسْمِ اللهِ الرَّحْمٰنِ الرَّحِيمِ ﴿١﴾

اَلْحَمْدُ لِلّٰهِ رَبِّ الْعَالَمِينَۙ ﴿٢﴾ اَلرَّحْمٰنِ الرَّحِيمِۙ ﴿٣﴾

مَالِكِ يَوْمِ الدِّينِۜ ﴿٤﴾

1. *Bismillāhi 'r-Raḥmāni 'r-Raḥīm.*
2. *Alḥamdulillāhi Rabbi 'l-ʿAlamīn.*
3. *Ar-Raḥmāni 'r-Raḥīm.*
4. *Māliki yawmi 'd-dīn.*

1. In the Name of Allāh, Most Gracious, Most Merciful.
2. All praise is due to Allāh, Lord of the Worlds.
3. Most Gracious, Most Merciful.
4. The Sovereign of the Day of Judgement.

(1:1-4)

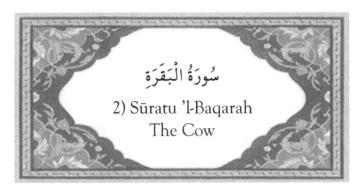

سُورَةُ الْبَقَرَةِ

2) Sūratu 'l-Baqarah
The Cow

بِسْمِ اللهِ الرَّحْمٰنِ الرَّحِيمِ

الٓمٓ ﴿١﴾ ذٰلِكَ الْكِتَابُ لَا رَيْبَۛ فِيهِۛ هُدًى لِلْمُتَّقِينَ ﴿٢﴾

Bismillāhi 'r-Raḥmāni 'r-Raḥīm.

1. *Alif. Lām. Mīm.*
2. *Dhālika 'l-kitābu lā rayba fīhi huda 'l-li 'l-muttaqīn.*

In the Name of Allāh, Most Gracious, Most Merciful.

1. *Alif. Lām. Mīm.*
2. This is the Book about which there is no doubt, a guidance for those conscious of Allāh.

(2:1-2)

سُورَةُ اٰلِ عِمْرٰنَ

3) Sūratu Āli ʿImrān, The Family of ʿImrān

بِسْمِ اللّٰهِ الرَّحْمٰنِ الرَّحِيمِ

الٓمٓ ﴿١﴾ اَللّٰهُ لَٓا اِلٰهَ اِلَّا هُوَۙ الْحَيُّ الْقَيُّومُۜ ﴿٢﴾

Bismillāhi 'r-Raḥmāni 'r-Raḥīm.

1. *Alif. Lām. Mīm.*
2. *Allāhu lā ilāha illā huwa 'l-ḥayyu 'l-qayyūm.*

In the Name of Allāh, Most Gracious, Most Merciful.

1. *Alif. Lām. Mīm.*
2. Allāh! There is no deity except Him, the Ever-Living, the Sustainer of Existence.

(3:1-2)

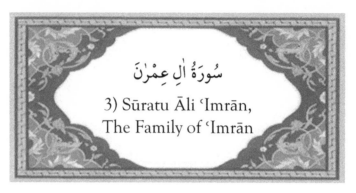

سُورَةُ النِّسَاءِ

4) Sūratu 'n-Nisā', The Women

بِسْمِ اللهِ الرَّحْمٰنِ الرَّحِيمِ

يَآ اَيُّهَا النَّاسُ اتَّقُوا رَبَّكُمُ الَّذٖى خَلَقَكُمْ مِنْ نَفْسٍ وَاحِدَةٍ

وَخَلَقَ مِنْهَا زَوْجَهَا وَبَثَّ مِنْهُمَا رِجَالًا كَثٖيرًا وَنِسَآءً وَاتَّقُوا اللّٰهَ

الَّذٖى تَسَآءَلُونَ بِهٖ وَالْاَرْحَامَ اِنَّ اللّٰهَ كَانَ عَلَيْكُمْ رَقٖيبًا ﴿١﴾

Bismillāhi 'r-Raḥmāni 'r-Raḥīm.

1. *Yā ayyuha 'n-nāsu 'ttaqqū rabbakumu 'Lladhī khalaqakum min nafsi 'w-wāḥidatiw-wa khalaqa minhā zawjahā wa baththa minhumā rijālan kathīran wa nisā'u wa 'ttaqū 'Llāha 'Lladhī tasā'alūna bihi wa 'l-arḥāma inna 'Llāha kāna ʿalaykum raqība.*

In the Name of Allāh, Most Gracious, Most Merciful.

1. O Mankind! Fear your Lord, Who created you from one soul and created from it its mate and dispersed from both of them many men

and women. And fear Allāh, through Whom you ask one another, and the wombs. Indeed, Allāh is ever, over you, an Observer.

(4:1)

سُورَةُ الْمَائِدَةِ

5) Sūratu 'l-Mā'idah, The Feast

بِسْمِ اللّٰهِ الرَّحْمٰنِ الرَّحِيمِ

يَا اَيُّهَا الَّذِينَ اٰمَنُوا اَوْفُوا بِالْعُقُودِ اُحِلَّتْ لَكُمْ بَهِيمَةُ

الْاَنْعَامِ اِلَّا مَا يُتْلٰى عَلَيْكُمْ غَيْرَ مُحِلِّى الصَّيْدِ وَاَنْتُمْ حُرُمٌ

اِنَّ اللّٰهَ يَحْكُمُ مَا يُرِيدُ ﴿١﴾

Bismillāhi 'r-Raḥmāni 'r-Raḥīm.

1. *Yā ayyuha 'Lladhīna āmanū awfū bi 'l-ʿuqūdi uḥillat lakum bahīmatu 'l-anʿāmi illā mā yutlā ʿalaykum ghayra muḥilli 'ṣ-ṣaydi wa antum ḥurumun inna 'Llāha yaḥkumu mā yurīd.*

In the Name of Allāh, Most Gracious, Most Merciful.

1. O you who have believed! Fulfill all obligations. Lawful for you (for food) are the animals of grazing livestock except for that which is recited to you (in this Qur'an), hunting not being permitted while you are in

the state of *iḥrām* (for Hajj or ʿ*Umrah*). Indeed, Allāh ordains what He intends.

(5:1)

سُورَةُ الْأَنْعَامِ

6) Sūratu 'l-An'ām, The Cattle

بِسْمِ اللهِ الرَّحْمٰنِ الرَّحِيمِ

اَلْحَمْدُ لِلّٰهِ الَّذِى خَلَقَ السَّمٰوَاتِ وَالْاَرْضَ وَجَعَلَ الظُّلُمَاتِ
وَالنُّورَ ثُمَّ الَّذِينَ كَفَرُوا بِرَبِّهِمْ يَعْدِلُونَ ﴿١﴾

Bismillāhi 'r-Raḥmāni 'r-Raḥīm.

1. *Alḥamdu lillāhi 'Lladhī khalaqa 's-samāwāti wa 'l-arḍa wa ja'ala 'ẓ-ẓulumāti wa 'n-nūr, thumma 'Lladhīna kafarū bi-rabbihim ya'dilūn.*

In the Name of Allāh, Most Gracious, Most Merciful.

1. All praise is due to Allāh, Who created the Heavens and the Earth and made the darkness and the light. Then those who disbelieve equate (others) with their Lord.

(6:1)

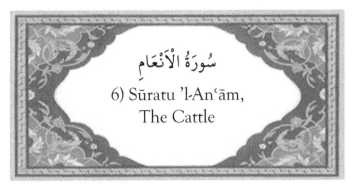

سُورَةُ الْأَعْرَافِ

7) Sūratu 'l-Aʿrāf, The Heights

بِسْمِ اللهِ الرَّحْمٰنِ الرَّحِيمِ

الٓمٓصٓ ﴿١﴾ كِتَابٌ أُنْزِلَ إِلَيْكَ فَلَا يَكُنْ فِى صَدْرِكَ حَرَجٌ
مِنْهُ لِتُنْذِرَ بِهِ وَذِكْرٰى لِلْمُؤْمِنِينَ ﴿٢﴾

Bismillāhi 'r-Raḥmāni 'r-Raḥīm.

1. *Alif. Lām. Mīm. Ṣād.*
2. *Kitābun unzila ilayka fa lā yakun fī saḍrika ḥarajum-minhu li tundhira bihi wa Dhikrā li 'l-mu'minīn.*

In the Name of Allāh, Most Gracious, Most Merciful.

1. *Alif. Lām. Mīm. Ṣād.*
2. (This is) a Book revealed to you, (O Muḥammad). So, let there not be in your heart distress therefrom, that you may warn thereby and as a reminder to the Believers.

(7:1-2)

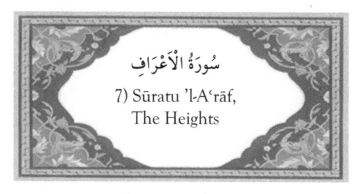

سُورَةُ الْأَنْفَالِ

8) Sūratu 'l-Anfāl, The Spoils

بِسْمِ اللهِ الرَّحْمٰنِ الرَّحِيمِ

يَسْـَٔلُونَكَ عَنِ الْأَنْفَالِ قُلِ الْأَنْفَالُ لِلّٰهِ وَالرَّسُولِ فَاتَّقُوا اللّٰهَ
وَأَصْلِحُوا ذَاتَ بَيْنِكُمْ وَأَطِيعُوا اللّٰهَ وَرَسُولَهُ إِنْ كُنْتُمْ
مُؤْمِنِينَ ﴿١﴾

Bismillāhi 'r-Raḥmāni 'r-Raḥīm.

1. *Yas-alūnaka ʿani 'l-anfāli quli 'l-anfālu lillāhi wa 'r-rasūli fattaqu 'Llāha wa aṣliḥū dhāta baynikum wa atīʿu 'Llāha wa rasūlahu in kuntum mu'minīn.*

In the Name of Allāh, Most Gracious, Most Merciful.

1. They ask you, (O Muḥammad), about the bounties (of war). Say, "The (decision concerning) bounties is for Allāh and the Messenger." So, fear Allāh and amend that

which is between you and obey Allāh and His
Messenger, if you should be believers.

(8:1)

سُورَةُ التَّوْبَةِ

9) Sūratu 't-Tawbah, Repentance

أَعُوذُ بِاللهِ مِنْ شَرِّ الْكُفَّارِ وَمِنْ غَضَبِ الجَبَّار الْعِزَّةِ لِلَّهِ
الْوَاحِدِ الْقَهَّارْ

بَرَآءَةٌ مِنَ اللهِ وَرَسُولِهِ إِلَى الَّذِينَ عَاهَدْتُمْ مِنَ الْمُشْرِكِينَ ﴿١﴾
فَسِيحُوا فِى الْأَرْضِ أَرْبَعَةَ أَشْهُرٍ وَاعْلَمُوا أَنَّكُمْ غَيْرُ
مُعْجِزِى اللهِ وَأَنَّ اللهَ مُخْزِى الْكَافِرِينَ ﴿٢﴾

Aʿūdhu billāhi min sharri 'l-kuffār wa min ghaḍabi 'l-jabbār al-ʿizzatu lillāhi 'l-wāḥidu 'l-qahhār.

1. *Barā'atun mina 'Llāhi wa rasūlihi ila 'Lladhīna ʿāhadtum mina 'l-mushrikīn.*
2. *Fasīḥū fi 'l-arḍi arbaʿata ashhurī wāʿlamū annakum ghayru muʿjizi 'Llāhi wa anna 'Llāha mukhzi 'l-kāfirīn.*

I seek refuge in Allāh from the evil of disbelievers and from the Anger of The Forceful One. Indeed, Majesty is for Allāh, The Only One, The Subduer.

1. Freedom from obligation (is proclaimed) from Allāh and His Messenger toward those of the idolaters with whom you made a treaty.
2. Travel freely in the land four months and know that you cannot escape Allāh and that Allāh will confound the disbelievers (in His Guidance).

(9:1-2)

سُورَةُ يُونُسَ

10) Sūrat Yūnus, Jonah

بِسْمِ اللّٰهِ الرَّحْمٰنِ الرَّحِيمِ

الٓرٰ تِلْكَ اٰيَاتُ الْكِتَابِ الْحَكِيمِ ﴿١﴾

Bismillāhi 'r-Raḥmāni 'r-Raḥīm.

1. *Alif. Lām. Rā. Tilka āyātu 'l-kitābi 'l-ḥakīm.*

In the Name of Allāh, Most Gracious, Most Merciful.

1. *Alif. Lām. Rā.* These are the verses of the Wise Book.

(10:1)

سُورَةُ هُودٍ

11) Sūrat Hūd, Hud

بِسْمِ اللهِ الرَّحْمٰنِ الرَّحِيمِ

الٓرٰ كِتَابٌ أُحْكِمَتْ اٰيَاتُهُ ثُمَّ فُصِّلَتْ مِنْ لَدُنْ حَكِيمٍ خَبِيرٍ ۙ ﴿١﴾

Bismillāhi 'r-Raḥmāni 'r-Raḥīm.

1. *Alif. Lām. Rā. Kitābun uḥkimat āyātuhu thumma fuṣṣilat mil-ladun ḥakīmin khabīr.*

In the Name of Allāh, Most Gracious, Most Merciful.

1. *Alif. Lām. Rā.* (This is) a Book whose verses are perfected and then presented in detail from (The One Who is) Wise and Acquainted. (11:1)

سُورَةُ يُوسُفَ

12) Sūrat Yūsuf, Joseph

بِسْمِ اللهِ الرَّحْمٰنِ الرَّحِيمِ

الٓرٰ تِلْكَ اٰيَاتُ الْكِتَابِ الْمُبِينِ ﴿١﴾

Bismillāhi 'r-Raḥmāni 'r-Raḥīm.

1. *Alif. Lām. Rā. Tilka āyātu 'l-kitābi 'l-mubīn.*

In the Name of Allāh, Most Gracious, Most Merciful.

1. *Alif. Lām. Rā.* These are the verses of the Clear Book.

(12:1)

سُورَةُ الرَّعْدِ

13) Sūratu 'r-Ra'd, The Thunder

بِسْمِ اللهِ الرَّحْمٰنِ الرَّحِيمِ

الٓمٓرٰ تِلْكَ اٰيَاتُ الْكِتَابِ وَالَّذِىٓ اُنْزِلَ اِلَيْكَ مِنْ رَبِّكَ الْحَقُّ
وَلٰكِنَّ اَكْثَرَ النَّاسِ لَا يُؤْمِنُونَ ﴿١﴾

Bismillāhi 'r-Raḥmāni 'r-Raḥīm.

1. *Alif. Lām. Mīm. Rā. Tilka āyātu 'l-kitābi wa 'Lladhī unzila ilayka mi 'r-rabbika 'l-ḥaqqu wa lākinna akthara 'n-nāsi lā yu'minūn.*

In the Name of Allāh, Most Gracious, Most Merciful.

1. *Alif. Lām. Mīm. Rā.* These are the verses of the Book, and what has been revealed to you from your Lord is the truth, but most of the people do not believe.

(13:1)

سُورَةُ إِبْرٰهِيمَ

14) Sūrat Ibrāhīm, Abraham

بِسْمِ اللهِ الرَّحْمٰنِ الرَّحِيمِ

الٓرٰ كِتَابٌ اَنْزَلْنَاهُ اِلَيْكَ لِتُخْرِجَ النَّاسَ مِنَ الظُّلُمَاتِ اِلَى
النُّورِ بِاِذْنِ رَبِّهِمْ اِلٰى صِرَاطِ الْعَزِيزِ الْحَمِيدِ ﴿١﴾

Bismillāhi 'r-Raḥmāni 'r-Raḥīm.

1. *Alif. Lām. Rā. Kitābun anzalnāhu ilayka li tukhrija 'n-nāsa mina 'ẓ-ẓulumāti ila 'n-nūri bi-idhni rabbihim ilā ṣirāṭi 'l-ʿazīzi 'l-ḥamīd.*

In the Name of Allāh, Most Gracious, Most Merciful.

1. *Alif. Lām. Rā.* (This is) a Book which We have revealed to you, (O Muḥammad), that you might bring Mankind out of darkness into the Light by permission of their Lord, to the path of the Exalted in Might, the Praiseworthy.

(14:1)

سُورَةُ الْحِجْرِ

15) Sūratu 'l-Ḥijr, The Rocky Tract

بِسْمِ اللهِ الرَّحْمٰنِ الرَّحِيمِ

الٓرۚ تِلْكَ اٰيَاتُ الْكِتَابِ وَقُرْاٰنٍ مُبِينٍ ﴿١﴾

Bismillāhi 'r-Raḥmāni 'r-Raḥīm.

1. *Alif. Lām. Rā. Tilka āyātu 'l-kitābi wa qur'āni 'm-mubīn.*

In the Name of Allāh, Most Gracious, Most Merciful.

1. *Alif. Lām. Rā.* These are the verses of the Book and a clear Qur'an.

(15:1)

سُورَةُ النَّحْلِ

16) Sūratu 'n-Naḥl, The Honey Bees

بِسْمِ اللّٰهِ الرَّحْمٰنِ الرَّحِيمِ

اَتٰى اَمْرُ اللّٰهِ فَلَا تَسْتَعْجِلُوهُ سُبْحَانَهُ وَتَعَالٰى عَمَّا يُشْرِكُونَ ﴿١﴾

Bismillāhi 'r-Raḥmāni 'r-Raḥīm.

1. *Atā amru 'Llāhi fa lā tastaʿjilūhu subḥānahū wa taʿalā ʿammā yushrikūn.*

In the Name of Allāh, Most Gracious, Most Merciful.

1. The command of Allāh is coming, so be not impatient for it. Exalted is He and high above what they associate with Him.

(16:1)

سُورَةُ الْإِسْرَاءِ

17) Sūratu 'l-Isrā', The Night Journey

بِسْمِ اللهِ الرَّحْمٰنِ الرَّحِيمِ

سُبْحَانَ الَّذِي أَسْرَىٰ بِعَبْدِهِ لَيْلًا مِنَ الْمَسْجِدِ الْحَرَامِ إِلَى الْمَسْجِدِ
الْأَقْصَا الَّذِي بَارَكْنَا حَوْلَهُ لِنُرِيَهُ مِنْ آيَاتِنَا إِنَّهُ هُوَ السَّمِيعُ الْبَصِيرُ ﴿١﴾

Bismillāhi 'r-Raḥmāni 'r-Raḥīm.

1. *Subḥāna 'Lladhī asrā bi ʿabdihi layla 'm-mina 'l-masjidi 'l-ḥarāmi ila 'l-masjidi 'l-aqṣa 'Lladhī bāraknā ḥawlahu li nuriyahu min āyātinā innahu huwa 's-samīʿu 'l-baṣīr.*

In the Name of Allāh, Most Gracious, Most Merciful.

1. Exalted is He Who took His Servant by night from the Sacred House to the most Far-Distant Mosque, whose surroundings We have blessed, to show him of Our Signs. Indeed, He is The Hearing, The Seeing.

(17:1)

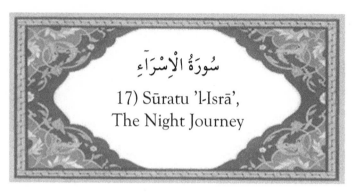

سُورَةُ الْكَهْفِ

18) Sūratu 'l-Kahf, The Cave

بِسْمِ اللهِ الرَّحْمٰنِ الرَّحِيمِ

اَلْحَمْدُ لِلّٰهِ الَّذِىٓ اَنْزَلَ عَلٰى عَبْدِهِ الْكِتَابَ

وَلَمْ يَجْعَلْ لَهُ عِوَجًا ﴿١﴾

Bismillāhi 'r-Raḥmāni 'r-Raḥīm.

1. *Alḥamdu lillāhi 'Lladhī anzala ʿalā ʿabdihi 'l-kitāba wa lam yajʿal lahu ʿiwajā.*

In the Name of Allāh, Most Gracious, Most Merciful.

1. (All) praise is (due) to Allāh, Who has sent down upon His Servant the Book and has not made therein any deviance.

(18:1)

سُورَةُ مَرْيَمَ

19) Sūrat Maryam, Mary

بِسْمِ اللهِ الرَّحْمٰنِ الرَّحِيمِ

كٓهيٓعٓصٓ ﴿١﴾ ذِكْرُ رَحْمَتِ رَبِّكَ عَبْدَهُۥ زَكَرِيَّآ ﴿٢﴾

إِذْ نَادَىٰ رَبَّهُۥ نِدَآءً خَفِيًّا ﴿٣﴾

Bismillāhi 'r-Raḥmāni 'r-Raḥīm.

1. *Kāf. Hā. Yā. ʿAyn. Sād.*
2. *Dhikru raḥmati rabbika ʿabdahu zakarīyyā.*
3. *Idh nādā rabbahu nidā'an khafiyyā.*

In the Name of Allāh, Most Gracious, Most Merciful.

1. *Kāf. Hā. Yā. ʿAyn. Ṣād.*
2. (This is) a mention of the Mercy of your Lord to His Servant Zakarīyyā.
3. When he called to his Lord a private supplication.

(19:1-3)

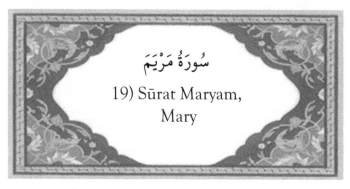

سُورَةُ طٰهٰ

20) Sūrat TāHā, Taha ﷺ

بِسْمِ اللّٰهِ الرَّحْمٰنِ الرَّحِيمِ

طٰهٰ ﴿١﴾ مَا أَنْزَلْنَا عَلَيْكَ الْقُرْاٰنَ لِتَشْقٰى ﴿٢﴾

Bismillāhi 'r-Raḥmāni 'r-Raḥīm.

1. *Ṭā. Hā.*
2. *Mā anzalnā 'alayka 'l-qur'āna li tashqā.*

In the Name of Allāh, Most Gracious, Most Merciful.

1. *Ṭā. Hā.*
2. We have not sent down to you the Qur'an that you be distressed.

(20:1-2)

سُورَةُ الْأَنْبِيَاءِ

21) Sūratu 'l-Anbiyā', The Prophets

بِسْمِ اللّٰهِ الرَّحْمٰنِ الرَّحِيمِ

اقْتَرَبَ لِلنَّاسِ حِسَابُهُمْ وَهُمْ فِى غَفْلَةٍ مُعْرِضُونَ ﴿١﴾

Bismillāhi 'r-Raḥmāni 'r-Raḥīm.

1. *Iqtaraba li 'n-nāsi ḥisābuhum wa hum fī ghaflati 'm-muʿriḍūn.*

In the Name of Allāh, Most Gracious, Most Merciful.

1. (The time of) their account has approached for the people, while they are in heedlessness turning away.

(21:1)

❁

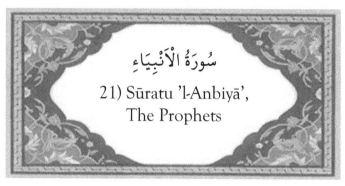

سُورَةُ الْحَجِّ

22) Sūratu 'l-Ḥajj, The Pilgrimage

بِسْمِ اللهِ الرَّحْمٰنِ الرَّحِيمِ

يَآ اَيُّهَا النَّاسُ اتَّقُوا رَبَّكُمْ اِنَّ زَلْزَلَةَ السَّاعَةِ شَيْءٌ عَظِيمٌ ﴿١﴾

Bismillāhi 'r-Raḥmāni 'r-Raḥīm.

1. *Yā ayyuha 'n-nāsu 'ttaqū rabbakum inna zalzalata 's-sā'ati shayy'un 'aẓīm.*

In the Name of Allāh, Most Gracious, Most Merciful.

1. O Mankind! Fear your Lord. Indeed, the convulsion of the (final) Hour is a terrible thing.

(22:1)

❁

سُورَةُ الْمُؤْمِنُونَ

23) Sūratu 'l-Mu'minūn, The Believers

بِسْمِ اللهِ الرَّحْمٰنِ الرَّحِيمِ

قَدْ اَفْلَحَ الْمُؤْمِنُونَۙ ﴿١﴾ اَلَّذِينَ هُمْ فِى صَلَاتِهِمْ خَاشِعُونَۙ ﴿٢﴾

Bismillāhi 'r-Raḥmāni 'r-Raḥīm.

1. *Qad aflaḥa 'l-mu'minūn.*
2. *Alladhīna hum fī ṣalātihim khāshiʿūn.*

In the Name of Allāh, Most Gracious, Most Merciful.

1. Certainly, will the Believers have succeeded:
2. They who are during their prayer humbly submissive.

(23:1-2)

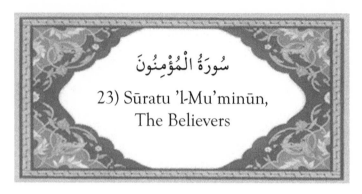

سُورَةُ النُّورِ

24) Sūratu 'n-Nūr, The Light

بِسْمِ اللهِ الرَّحْمٰنِ الرَّحِيمِ

سُورَةٌ اَنْزَلْنَاهَا وَفَرَضْنَاهَا وَاَنْزَلْنَا فِيهَآ اٰيَاتٍ بَيِّنَاتٍ لَعَلَّكُمْ
تَذَكَّرُونَ ﴿١﴾

Bismillāhi 'r-Raḥmāni 'r-Raḥīm.

1. *Sūratun anzalnāhā wa faraḍnāhā wa anzalnā fīhā āyāti 'm-bayyināti 'l-laʿallakum tadhakkarūn.*

In the Name of Allāh, Most Gracious, Most Merciful.

1. (This is) a *sūrah* which We have sent down and made (that within it) obligatory and revealed therein verses of clear evidence that you might remember.

(24:1)

سُورَةُ الْفُرْقَانِ

25) Sūratu 'l-Furqān, The Criterion

بِسْمِ اللهِ الرَّحْمٰنِ الرَّحِيمِ

تَبَارَكَ الَّذِى نَزَّلَ الْفُرْقَانَ عَلٰى عَبْدِهٖ لِيَكُونَ

لِلْعَالَمِينَ نَذِيرًا ﴿١﴾

Bismillāhi 'r-Raḥmāni 'r-Raḥīm.

1. *Tabāraka 'Lladhī nazzala 'l-furqāna ʿalā ʿabdihi li yakūna li 'l-ʿalamīna nadhīrā.*

In the Name of Allāh, Most Gracious, Most Merciful.

1. Blessed is He who sent down the Criterion upon His Servant that he may be to the Worlds a warner.

(25:1)

سُورَةُ الشُّعَرَاءِ

26) Sūratu 'sh-Shuʿarā, The Poets

بِسْمِ اللهِ الرَّحْمٰنِ الرَّحِيمِ

طٰسٓمٓ ﴿١﴾ تِلْكَ اٰيَاتُ الْكِتَابِ الْمُبِينِ ﴿٢﴾

Bismillāhi 'r-Raḥmāni 'r-Raḥīm.

1. *Ṭā. Sīn. Mīm.*
2. *Tilka āyātu 'l-kitābi 'l-mubīn.*

In the Name of Allāh, Most Gracious, Most Merciful.

1. *Ṭā. Sīn. Mīm.*
2. These are the verses of the Clear Book.

(26:1-2)

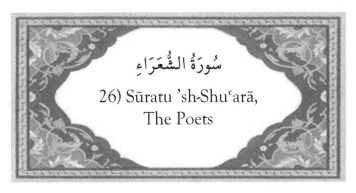

سُورَةُ النَّمْلِ

27) Sūratu 'n-Naml, The Ants

بِسْمِ اللهِ الرَّحْمٰنِ الرَّحِيمِ

طٰسٓ تِلْكَ اٰيَاتُ الْقُرْاٰنِ وَكِتَابٍ مُبِينٍ ﴿١﴾

Bismillāhi 'r-Raḥmāni 'r-Raḥīm.

1. *Ṭā. Sīn. Tilka āyātu 'l-qur'āni wa kitābi 'm-mubīn.*

In the Name of Allāh, Most Gracious, Most Merciful.

1. *Ṭā. Sīn*. These are the verses of the Qur'an and a Clear Book.

(27:1)

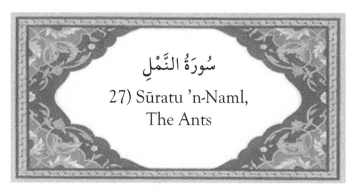

سُورَةُ الْقَصَصِ

28) Sūratu 'l-Qaṣaṣ, The Stories

بِسْمِ اللهِ الرَّحْمٰنِ الرَّحِيمِ

طٰسٓمٓ ﴿١﴾ تِلْكَ اٰيَاتُ الْكِتَابِ الْمُبِينِ ﴿٢﴾

Bismillāhi 'r-Raḥmāni 'r-Raḥīm.

1. *Ṭā. Sīn. Mīm.*
2. *Tilka āyātu 'l-kitābi 'l-mubīn.*

In the Name of Allāh, Most Gracious, Most Merciful.

1. *Ṭā. Sīn. Mīm.*
2. These are the verses of the Clear Book.

(28:1)

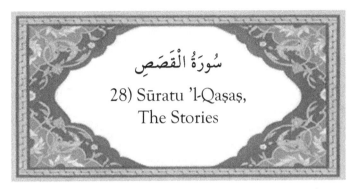

سُورَةُ الْعَنْكَبُوتِ

29) Sūratu 'l-'Ankabūt, The Spider

بِسْمِ اللّٰهِ الرَّحْمٰنِ الرَّحِيمِ

الٓمٓ ﴿١﴾ أَحَسِبَ النَّاسُ أَنْ يُتْرَكُوٓا أَنْ يَقُولُوٓا

اٰمَنَّا وَهُمْ لَا يُفْتَنُونَ ﴿٢﴾

Bismillāhi 'r-Raḥmāni 'r-Raḥīm.

1. *Alif. Lām. Mīm.*
2. *A-ḥasiba 'n-nāsu ayyutrakū ay-yaqūlū āmannā wa hum lā yuftanūn.*

In the Name of Allāh, Most Gracious, Most Merciful.

1. *Alif. Lām. Mīm.*
2. Do the people think that they will be left to say, "We believe" and they will not be tried?

(29:1-2)

سُورَةُ الرُّومِ

30) Sūratu 'r-Rūm, Rome

بِسْمِ اللهِ الرَّحْمٰنِ الرَّحِيمِ

الٓمٓ ﴿١﴾ غُلِبَتِ الرُّومُ ﴿٢﴾

فِيٓ أَدْنَى الْأَرْضِ وَهُمْ مِنْ بَعْدِ غَلَبِهِمْ سَيَغْلِبُونَ ﴿٣﴾

Bismillāhi 'r-Raḥmāni 'r-Raḥīm.

1. *Alif. Lām. Mīm.*
2. *Ghulibati 'r-rūm.*
3. *Fī adna 'l-arḍi wa hum mim-ba'di ghalabihim sa-yaghlibūn.*

In the Name of Allāh, Most Gracious, Most Merciful.

1. *Alif. Lām. Mīm.*
2. The Byzantines have been defeated,
3. In the nearest land, but they, after their defeat, will overcome.

(30:1-3)

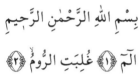

سُورَةُ لُقْمَانَ

31) Sūrat Luqmān, Luqman

بِسْمِ اللهِ الرَّحْمٰنِ الرَّحِيمِ

الٓمٓ ﴿١﴾ تِلْكَ اٰيَاتُ الْكِتَابِ الْحَكِيمِۙ ﴿٢﴾

Bismillāhi 'r-Raḥmāni 'r-Raḥīm.

1. *Alif. Lām. Mīm.*
2. *Tilka āyātu 'l-kitābi 'l-ḥakīm.*

In the Name of Allāh, Most Gracious, Most Merciful.

1. *Alif. Lām. Mīm.*
2. These are verses of the Wise Book.

(31:1-2)

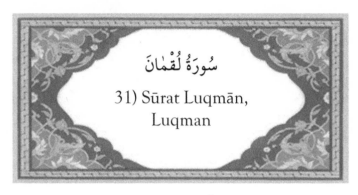

سُورَةُ السَّجْدَةِ

32) Sūrat as-Sajdah, The Prostration

بِسْمِ اللَّهِ الرَّحْمَٰنِ الرَّحِيمِ

الٓمٓ ﴿١﴾ تَنزِيلُ الْكِتَابِ لَا رَيْبَ فِيهِ مِن رَّبِّ الْعَالَمِينَ ﴿٢﴾

Bismillāhi 'r-Raḥmāni 'r-Raḥīm.

1. *Alif. Lām. Mīm.*
2. *Tanzīlu 'l-kitābi lā rayba fīhi mir-rabbi 'l-ʿālamīn.*

In the Name of Allāh, Most Gracious, Most Merciful.

1. *Alif. Lām. Mīm.*
2. (This is) the revelation of the Book about which there is no doubt from the Lord of the Worlds.

(32:1-2)

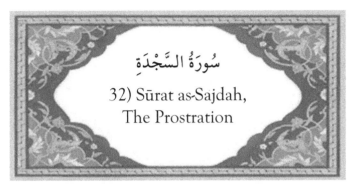

سُورَةُ الْاَحْزَابِ

33) Sūratu 'l-Aḥzāb, The Clans

بِسْمِ اللّٰهِ الرَّحْمٰنِ الرَّحِيمِ

يَٓا اَيُّهَا النَّبِيُّ اتَّقِ اللّٰهَ وَلَا تُطِعِ الْكَافِرِينَ وَالْمُنَافِقِينَۜ

اِنَّ اللّٰهَ كَانَ عَلِيمًا حَكِيمًاۙ ﴿١﴾

Bismillāhi 'r-Raḥmāni 'r-Raḥīm.

1. *Yā ayyuha 'n-nabīyyu 'ttaqi 'Llāha wa lā tutiʿi 'l-kāfirīna wa 'l-munāfiqīna inna 'Llāha kāna ʿalīman ḥakīmā.*

In the Name of Allāh, Most Gracious, Most Merciful.

1. O Prophet, fear Allāh and do not obey the disbelievers and the hypocrites. Indeed, Allāh is Ever-Knowing and Wise.

(33:1)

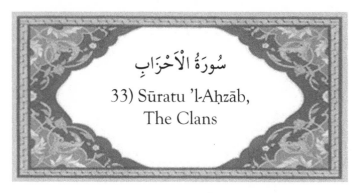

سُورَةُ سَبَإٍ

34) Sūrat Sabā', Sheba

بِسْمِ اللهِ الرَّحْمٰنِ الرَّحِيمِ

اَلْحَمْدُ لِلّٰهِ الَّذِى لَهُ مَا فِى السَّمٰوَاتِ وَمَا فِى الْاَرْضِ وَلَهُ
الْحَمْدُ فِى الْاٰخِرَةِ وَهُوَ الْحَكِيمُ الْخَبِيرُ ﴿١﴾

Bismillāhi 'r-Raḥmāni 'r-Raḥīm.

1. *Alḥamduli Llāhi 'Lladhī lahu mā fi 's-samāwāti wa mā fi 'l-arḍi wa lahu 'l-ḥamdu fi 'l-ākhirati wa huwa 'l-ḥakīmu 'l-khabīr.*

In the Name of Allāh, Most Gracious, Most Merciful.

1. (All) praise is (due) to Allāh, to Whom belongs whatever is in the Heavens and whatever is in the Earth, and to Him belongs (all) praise in the Hereafter. And He is The Wise, The Acquainted.

(34:1)

سُورَةُ فَاطِرٍ

35) Sūrat Fāṭir, The Originator

بِسْمِ اللّٰهِ الرَّحْمٰنِ الرَّحِيمِ

اَلْحَمْدُ لِلّٰهِ فَاطِرِ السَّمٰوَاتِ وَالْاَرْضِ جَاعِلِ الْمَلٰٓئِكَةِ رُسُلًا
اُولٖٓى اَجْنِحَةٍ مَثْنٰى وَثُلٰثَ وَرُبَاعَ يَزِيدُ فِى الْخَلْقِ مَا يَشَٓاءُ
اِنَّ اللّٰهَ عَلٰى كُلِّ شَيْءٍ قَدِيرٌ ﴿١﴾

Bismillāhi 'r-Raḥmāni 'r-Raḥīm.

1. *Alḥamdu lillāhi fāṭiri 's-samāwāti wa 'l-arḍi jāʿili 'l-malā'ikati rusulan ulī ajniḥati 'm-mathnā wa thulātha wa rubāʿa yazīdu fi 'l-khalqi mā yashā'u inna 'Llāha ʿalā kulli shay-in qadīr.*

In the Name of Allāh, Most Gracious, Most Merciful.

1. (All) praise is (due) to Allāh, Creator of the Heavens and the Earth, (Who) made the angels messengers having wings, two or three or four. He increases in creation

what He wills. Indeed, Allāh is over all things competent.

(35:1)

سُورَةُ يٰسٓ

36) Sūrat YāSīn, Yasin ﷺ

بِسْمِ اللّٰهِ الرَّحْمٰنِ الرَّحِيمِ

يٰسٓ ﴿١﴾ وَالْقُرْاٰنِ الْحَكِيمِۙ ﴿٢﴾ اِنَّكَ لَمِنَ الْمُرْسَلِينَۙ ﴿٣﴾

عَلٰى صِرَاطٍ مُسْتَقِيمٍۜ ﴿٤﴾

Bismillāhi 'r-Raḥmāni 'r-Raḥīm.

1. *Yā. Sīn.*
2. *Wa 'l-qur'āni 'l-ḥakīm.*
3. *Innaka la mina 'l-mursalīn.*
4. *ʿAlā ṣirāṭi 'm-mustaqīm.*

In the Name of Allāh, Most Gracious, Most Merciful.

1. *Yā. Sīn.*
2. By the Wise Qur'an.
3. Indeed you, (O Muḥammad), are from among the messengers,
4. On a Straight Path.

(36:1-4)

سُورَةُ الصَّافَّاتِ

37) Sūratu 'ṣ-Ṣaffāt, Those in Ranks

بِسْمِ اللهِ الرَّحْمٰنِ الرَّحِيمِ

وَالصَّافَّاتِ صَفًّا ﴿١﴾ فَالزَّاجِرَاتِ زَجْرًا ﴿٢﴾

Bismillāhi 'r-Raḥmāni 'r-Raḥīm.

1. *Wa 'ṣ-ṣāffāti ṣaffā.*
2. *Fa 'z-zājirāti zajrā.*

In the Name of Allāh, Most Gracious, Most Merciful.

1. By those (angels) lined up in rows.
2. And those who drive (the clouds).

(37:1-2)

سُورَةُ صٓ

38) Sūrat Ṣād, Ṣād

بِسْمِ اللهِ الرَّحْمٰنِ الرَّحِيمِ

صٓ وَالْقُرْاٰنِ ذِى الذِّكْرِ ﴿١﴾

بَلِ الَّذِينَ كَفَرُوا فِى عِزَّةٍ وَشِقَاقٍ ﴿٢﴾

Bismillāhi 'r-Raḥmāni 'r-Raḥīm.

1. *Ṣād. Wa 'l-qur'āni 'dh-Dhikr.*
2. *Bali 'Lladhīna kafarū fī ʿizzatiwwa shiqāq.*

In the Name of Allāh, Most Gracious, Most Merciful.

1. *Ṣād*. By the Qur'an containing a reminder.
2. But those who disbelieve are in pride and dissension.

(38:1-2)

سُورَةُ الزُّمَرِ

39) Sūratu 'z-Zumar, The Crowds

بِسْمِ اللهِ الرَّحْمٰنِ الرَّحِيمِ

تَنْزِيلُ الْكِتَابِ مِنَ اللهِ الْعَزِيزِ الْحَكِيمِ ﴿١﴾

Bismillāhi 'r-Raḥmāni 'r-Raḥīm.

1. *Tanzīlu 'l-kitābi mina 'Llāhi 'l-'azīzi 'l-ḥakīm.*

In the Name of Allāh, Most Gracious, Most Merciful.

1. The revelation of the Qur'an is from Allāh, The Exalted in Might, The Wise.

(39:1)

❁

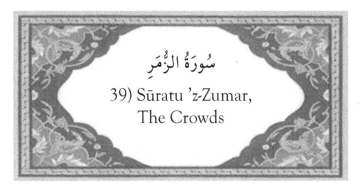

سُورَةُ الْمُؤْمِنِ

40) Sūratu 'l-Mu'min, The Believer

بِسْمِ اللهِ الرَّحْمٰنِ الرَّحِيمِ

حٰمٓ ﴿١﴾ تَنْزِيلُ الْكِتَابِ مِنَ اللهِ الْعَزِيزِ الْعَلِيمِ ﴿٢﴾

Bismillāhi 'r-Raḥmāni 'r-Raḥīm.

1. *Ḥā. Mīm.*
2. *Tanzīlu 'l-kitābi mina 'Llāhi 'l-ʿazīzi 'l-ʿalīm.*

In the Name of Allāh, Most Gracious, Most Merciful.

1. *Ḥā. Mīm.*
2. The revelation of the Book is from Allāh, The Exalted in Might, The Knowing.

(40:2)

سُورَةُ فُصِّلَتْ

41) Sūrat Fuṣṣilat, Explained in Detail

بِسْمِ اللهِ الرَّحْمٰنِ الرَّحِيمِ

حٰمٓ ﴿١﴾ تَنْزِيلٌ مِنَ الرَّحْمٰنِ الرَّحِيمِ ﴿٢﴾

Bismillāhi 'r-Raḥmāni 'r-Raḥīm.

1. *Ḥā. Mīm.*
2. *Tanzīlu 'm-mina 'r-raḥmāni 'r-raḥīm.*

In the Name of Allāh, Most Gracious, Most Merciful.

1. *Ḥā. Mīm.*
2. (This is) a revelation from The Most Gracious, Most Merciful.

(41:1-2)

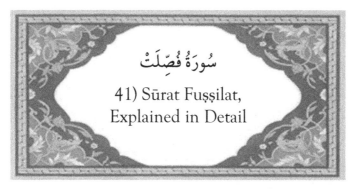

سُورَةُ الشُّورٰى

42) Sūratu 'sh-Shūrā, The Consultation

بِسْمِ اللهِ الرَّحْمٰنِ الرَّحِيمِ

حٰمٓ ﴿١﴾ عٓسٓقٓ ﴿٢﴾ كَذٰلِكَ يُوحِيٓ إِلَيْكَ وَإِلَى الَّذِينَ مِنْ
قَبْلِكَ اللهُ الْعَزِيزُ الْحَكِيمُ ﴿٣﴾

Bismillāhi 'r-Raḥmāni 'r-Raḥīm.

1. *Ḥā. Mīm.*
2. *'Ayn. Sīn. Qāf.*
3. *Kadhālika yūḥīyy ilayka wa ila 'Lladhīna min qablika 'Llāhu 'l-'azīzu 'l-ḥakīm.*

In the Name of Allāh, Most Gracious, Most Merciful.

1. *Ḥā. Mīm.*
2. *'Ayn. Sīn. Qāf.*
3. Thus has He revealed to you, (O Muḥammad), and to those before you, Allāh, The Exalted in Might, The Wise.

(42:1-3)

سُورَةُ الزُّخْرُفِ

43) Sūratu 'z-Zukhruf, The Ornaments

بِسْمِ اللهِ الرَّحْمٰنِ الرَّحِيمِ

حٰمٓ ﴿١﴾ وَالْكِتَابِ الْمُبِينِ ﴿٢﴾

Bismillāhi 'r-Raḥmāni 'r-Raḥīm.

1. *Ḥā. Mīm.*
2. *Wa 'l-kitābi 'l-mubīn.*

In the Name of Allāh, Most Gracious, Most Merciful.

1. Ḥā. Mīm.
2. By the Clear Book.

(43:1-2)

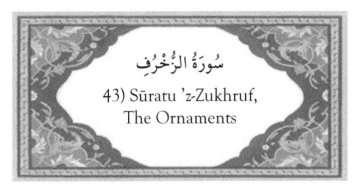

سُورَةُ الدُّخَانِ

44) Sūratu 'd-Dukhān, The Smoke

بِسْمِ اللهِ الرَّحْمٰنِ الرَّحِيمِ

حٰمٓ ﴿١﴾ وَالْكِتَابِ الْمُبِينِ ﴿٢﴾

Bismillāhi 'r-Raḥmāni 'r-Raḥīm.

1. *Ḥā. Mīm.*
2. *Wa 'l-kitābi 'l-mubīn.*

In the Name of Allāh, Most Gracious, Most Merciful.

1. Ḥā. Mīm.
2. By the Clear Book,

(44:1-2)

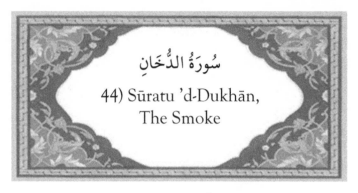

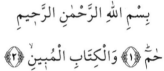

سُورَةُ الْجَاثِيَةِ

45) Sūratu 'l-Jāthiyah, The Kneeling Down

بِسْمِ اللهِ الرَّحْمٰنِ الرَّحِيمِ

حٰمٓ ﴿١﴾ تَنْزِيلُ الْكِتَابِ مِنَ اللهِ الْعَزِيزِ الْحَكِيمِ ﴿٢﴾

Bismillāhi 'r-Raḥmāni 'r-Raḥīm.

1. *Ḥā. Mīm.*
2. *Tanzīlu 'l-kitābi mina 'Llāhi 'l-'azīzi 'l-ḥakīm.*

In the Name of Allāh, Most Gracious, Most Merciful.

1. *Ḥā. Mīm.*
2. The revelation of the Book is from Allāh, The Exalted in Might, The Wise.

(45:1-2)

سُورَةُ الْأَحْقَافِ

46) Sūratu 'l-Aḥqāf, The Sand Dunes

بِسْمِ اللهِ الرَّحْمٰنِ الرَّحِيمِ

حٰمٓ ﴿١﴾ تَنْزِيلُ الْكِتَابِ مِنَ اللهِ الْعَزِيزِ الْحَكِيمِ ﴿٢﴾

Bismillāhi 'r-Raḥmāni 'r-Raḥīm.

1. *Ḥā. Mīm.*
2. *Tanzīlu 'l-kitābi mina 'Llāhi 'l-'azīzi 'l-ḥakīm.*

In the Name of Allāh, Most Gracious, Most Merciful.

1. *Ḥā. Mīm.*
2. The revelation of the Book is from Allāh, the Exalted in Might, The Wise.

(46:1-2)

سُورَةُ مُحَمَّدٍ

47) Sūrat Muḥammad, Muḥammad ﷺ

بِسْمِ اللهِ الرَّحْمٰنِ الرَّحِيمِ

اَلَّذِينَ كَفَرُوا وَصَدُّوا عَنْ سَبِيلِ اللهِ اَضَلَّ اَعْمَالَهُمْ ﴿١﴾

Bismillāhi 'r-Raḥmāni 'r-Raḥīm.

1. *Alladhīna kafarū wa ṣaddū ʿan sabīli 'Llāhi aḍalla aʿmālahum.*

In the Name of Allāh, Most Gracious, Most Merciful.

1. Those who disbelieve and avert (people) from the Way of Allāh, He will waste their deeds.

(47:1)

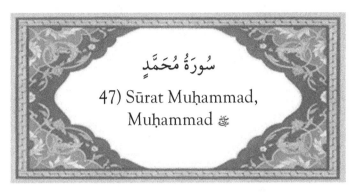

سُورَةُ الْفَتْحِ

48) Sūratu 'l-Fatḥ, The Conquest

بِسْمِ اللهِ الرَّحْمٰنِ الرَّحِيمِ

إِنَّا فَتَحْنَا لَكَ فَتْحًا مُبِينًا ﴿١﴾

Bismillāhi 'r-Raḥmāni 'r-Raḥīm.

1. *Innā fataḥnā laka fat-ḥam-mubīna.*

In the Name of Allāh, Most Gracious, Most Merciful.

1. Indeed, We have given you, (O Muḥammad), a clear conquest

(48:1)

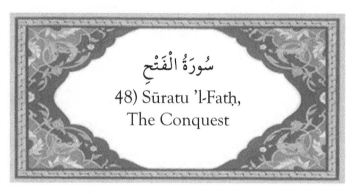

سُورَةُ الْحُجُرَاتِ

49) Sūratu 'l-Ḥujurāt, The Private Quarters

بِسْمِ اللّٰهِ الرَّحْمٰنِ الرَّحِيمِ

يَا اَيُّهَا الَّذِينَ اٰمَنُوا لَا تُقَدِّمُوا بَيْنَ يَدَيِ اللّٰهِ وَرَسُولِهِ وَاتَّقُوا
اللّٰهَ اِنَّ اللّٰهَ سَمِيعٌ عَلِيمٌ ﴿١﴾

Bismillāhi 'r-Raḥmāni 'r-Raḥīm.

1. *Yā ayyuha 'Lladhīna āmanū lā tuqaddimū bayna yadayi 'Llāhi wa rasūlihi wa 'ttaqū 'Llāha inna 'Llāha samī'un 'alīm.*

In the Name of Allāh, Most Gracious, Most Merciful.

1. O you who have believed, do not put (yourselves) before Allāh and His Messenger but fear Allāh. Indeed, Allāh is Hearing and Knowing.

(49:1)

سُورَةُ قٓ

50) Sūrat Qāf, Qāf

بِسْمِ اللهِ الرَّحْمٰنِ الرَّحِيمِ

قٓ وَالْقُرْاٰنِ الْمَجِيدِ ﴿١﴾ بَلْ عَجِبُوٓا اَنْ جَٓاءَهُمْ مُنْذِرٌ مِنْهُمْ
فَقَالَ الْكَافِرُونَ هٰذَا شَيْءٌ عَجِيبٌ ﴿٢﴾

Bismillāhi 'r-Raḥmāni 'r-Raḥīm.

1. *Qāf. Wa 'l-qur'āni 'l-majīd.*
2. *Bal ʿajibū an jā-ahum mundhiru 'm-minhum fa qāla 'l-kāfirūna hādhā shay-un ʿajīb.*

In the Name of Allāh, Most Gracious, Most Merciful.

1. *Qāf.* By the Honored Qur'an.
2. But they wonder that there has come to them a warner from among themselves, and the disbelievers say, "This is an amazing thing."

(50:1-2)

سُورَةُ الذَّارِيَاتِ

51) Sūratu 'dh-Dhārīyāt, The Scattering Winds

بِسْمِ اللهِ الرَّحْمٰنِ الرَّحِيمِ

وَالذَّارِيَاتِ ذَرْواً ﴿١﴾ فَالْحَامِلَاتِ وِقْراً ﴿٢﴾

Bismillāhi 'r-Raḥmāni 'r-Raḥīm.

1. *Wa 'dh-dhāriyāti dharwā.*
2. *Fa 'l-ḥāmilāti wiqrā.*

In the Name of Allāh, Most Gracious, Most Merciful.

1. By those (winds) scattering (dust) dispersing.
2. And those (clouds) carrying a load (of water).

(51:1-2)

۞

سُورَةُ الطُّورِ

52) Sūratu 'ṭ-Ṭūr, The Mount Sinai

بِسْمِ اللهِ الرَّحْمٰنِ الرَّحِيمِ

وَالطُّورِ ﴿١﴾ وَكِتَابٍ مَسْطُورٍ ﴿٢﴾

Bismillāhi 'r-Raḥmāni 'r-Raḥīm.

1. *Wa 'ṭ-ṭūr.*
2. *Wa kitābi 'm-masṭūr.*

In the Name of Allāh, Most Gracious, Most Merciful.

1. By the Mount (Sinai).
2. And (by) a Book inscribed.

(52:1-2)

سُورَةُ النَّجْمِ

53) Sūratu 'n-Najm, The Star

بِسْمِ اللَّهِ الرَّحْمَٰنِ الرَّحِيمِ

وَالنَّجْمِ إِذَا هَوَىٰ ﴿١﴾ مَا ضَلَّ صَاحِبُكُمْ وَمَا غَوَىٰ ﴿٢﴾

Bismillāhi 'r-Raḥmāni 'r-Raḥīm.

1. *Wa 'n-najmi idhā hawā.*
2. *Mā ḍalla ṣāḥibukum wa mā ghawā.*

In the Name of Allāh, Most Gracious, Most Merciful.

1. By the star when it descends.
2. Your Companion (Muḥammad) has not strayed, nor has he erred.

(53:1-2)

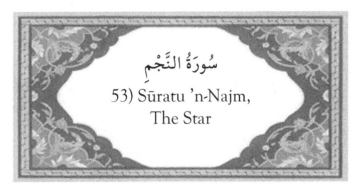

سُورَةُ الْقَمَرِ

54) Sūratu 'l-Qamar, The Moon

بِسْمِ اللهِ الرَّحْمٰنِ الرَّحِيمِ

اِقْتَرَبَتِ السَّاعَةُ وَانْشَقَّ الْقَمَرُ ﴿١﴾

Bismillāhi 'r-Raḥmāni 'r-Raḥīm.

1. *Iqtarabati 's-sāʿatu wa 'n-shaqqa 'l-qamar.*

In the Name of Allāh, Most Gracious, Most Merciful.

1. The Hour has come near, and the moon has split (in two).

(54:1)

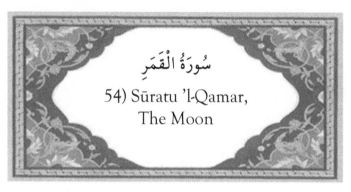

سُورَةُ الرَّحْمٰنِ

55) Sūratu 'r-Raḥmān, The Most Merciful

بِسْمِ اللّٰهِ الرَّحْمٰنِ الرَّحِيمِ

اَلرَّحْمٰنُۙ ﴿١﴾ عَلَّمَ الْقُرْاٰنَۜ ﴿٢﴾ خَلَقَ الْاِنْسَانَۙ ﴿٣﴾

عَلَّمَهُ الْبَيَانَ ﴿٤﴾

Bismillāhi 'r-Raḥmāni 'r-Raḥīm.

1. *Ar-Raḥmān.*
2. *'Allama 'l-Qur'ān.*
3. *Khalaqa 'l-insān.*
4. *'Allamahu 'l-bayān.*

In the Name of Allāh, Most Gracious, Most Merciful.

1. The Most Merciful
2. Taught the Qur'an,
3. Created Man,
4. (And) taught him eloquence.

(55:1-4)

سُورَةُ الْوَاقِعَةِ

56) Sūratu 'l-Wāqiʿah, The Occurrence

بِسْمِ اللهِ الرَّحْمٰنِ الرَّحِيمِ

إِذَا وَقَعَتِ الْوَاقِعَةُ ﴿١﴾ لَيْسَ لِوَقْعَتِهَا كَاذِبَةٌ ﴿٢﴾

خَافِضَةٌ رَّافِعَةٌ ﴿٣﴾

Bismillāhi 'r-Raḥmāni 'r-Raḥīm.

1. *Idhā waqaʿati 'l-wāqiʿah.*
2. *Laysa li waqʿatihā kādhibah.*
3. *Khāfidatu 'r-rāfiʿa.*

In the Name of Allāh, Most Gracious, Most Merciful.

1. When the Occurrence occurs,
2. There is, at its occurrence, no denial.
3. It will bring down (some) and raise up (others).

(56:1-3)

❁

سُورَةُ الْحَدِيدِ

57) Sūratu 'l-Ḥadīd, The Iron

بِسْمِ اللهِ الرَّحْمٰنِ الرَّحِيمِ

سَبَّحَ لِلّٰهِ مَا فِى السَّمٰوَاتِ وَالْأَرْضِ وَهُوَ الْعَزِيزُ الْحَكِيمُ ﴿١﴾

Bismillāhi 'r-Raḥmāni 'r-Raḥīm.

1. *Sabbaḥa lillāhi mā fi 's-samāwāti wa 'l-arḍi wa huwa 'l-ʿazīzu 'l-ḥakīm.*

In the Name of Allāh, Most Gracious, Most Merciful.

1. Whatever is in the Heavens and Earth exalts Allāh, and He is The Exalted in Might, The Wise.

(57:1)

سُورَةُ الْمُجَادَلَةِ

58) Sūratu 'l-Mujādilah, The Pleading

بِسْمِ اللهِ الرَّحْمٰنِ الرَّحِيمِ

قَدْ سَمِعَ اللهُ قَوْلَ الَّتِى تُجَادِلُكَ فِى زَوْجِهَا وَتَشْتَكِى إِلَى
اللهِ وَاللهُ يَسْمَعُ تَحَاوُرَكُمَا إِنَّ اللهَ سَمِيعٌ بَصِيرٌ ﴿١﴾

Bismillāhi 'r-Raḥmāni 'r-Raḥīm.

1. *Qad samiʿa 'Llāhu qawlallatī tujādiluka fī zawjihā wa tashtakī ila 'Llāhi wa 'Llāhu yasmaʿu taḥāwurakumā inna 'Llāha samīʿum-baṣīr.*

In the Name of Allāh, Most Gracious, Most Merciful.

1. Allāh has indeed heard (and accepted) the statement of the woman who pleads with you concerning her husband and carries her complaint (in prayer) to Allāh. And Allāh always hears the arguments between both sides among you. For, Allāh is All-Hearing and All-Seeing.

(58:1)

سُورَةُ الْحَشْرِ

59) Sūratu 'l-Ḥashr, The Gathering

بِسْمِ اللهِ الرَّحْمٰنِ الرَّحِيمِ

سَبَّحَ لِلّٰهِ مَا فِى السَّمٰوَاتِ وَمَا فِى الْاَرْضِۚ

وَهُوَ الْعَزِيزُ الْحَكِيمُ ﴿١﴾

Bismillāhi 'r-Raḥmāni 'r-Raḥīm.

1. *Sabbaḥa lillāhi mā fi 's-samāwāti wa mā fi 'l-arḍi wa huwa 'l-ʿazīzu 'l-ḥakīm.*

In the Name of Allāh, Most Gracious, Most Merciful.

1. Whatever is in the Heavens and whatever is on the Earth exalts Allāh, and He is The Exalted in Might, The Wise.

(59:1)

سُورَةُ الْمُمْتَحِنَةِ

60) Sūratu 'l-Mumtaḥinah, The Examined One

بِسْمِ اللّٰهِ الرَّحْمٰنِ الرَّحِيمِ

يَآ اَيُّهَا الَّذِينَ اٰمَنُوا لَا تَتَّخِذُوا عَدُوِّى وَعَدُوَّكُمْ اَوْلِيَآءَ تُلْقُونَ
اِلَيْهِمْ بِالْمَوَدَّةِ وَقَدْ كَفَرُوا بِمَا جَآءَكُمْ مِنَ الْحَقِّ يُخْرِجُونَ
الرَّسُولَ وَاِيَّاكُمْ اَنْ تُؤْمِنُوا بِاللّٰهِ رَبِّكُمْ اِنْ كُنْتُمْ خَرَجْتُمْ
جِهَادًا فِى سَبِيلِى وَابْتِغَآءَ مَرْضَاتِى تُسِرُّونَ اِلَيْهِمْ بِالْمَوَدَّةِ
وَاَنَا اَعْلَمُ بِمَآ اَخْفَيْتُمْ وَمَآ اَعْلَنْتُمْ وَمَنْ يَفْعَلْهُ مِنْكُمْ فَقَدْ
ضَلَّ سَوَآءَ السَّبِيلِ ﴿١﴾

Bismillāhi 'r-Raḥmāni 'r-Raḥīm.

1. *Yā ayyuha 'Lladhīna āmanū lā tattakhidhū ʿaduwwī wa ʿaduwwakum awlīyā-a tulqūna ilayhim bi 'l-mawaddati wa qad kafarū bi mā jā-akum mina 'l-ḥaqqi yukhrijūna 'r-rasūla wa iyyākum an tu'minū bi 'Llāhi rabbikum in kuntum kharajtum jihādan fī sabīlī wabtighā-*

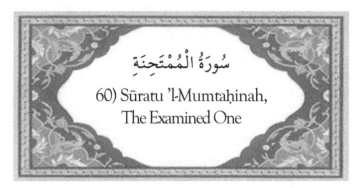

a marḍātī tusirrūna ilayhim bi 'l-mawaddati wa ana āʿalamu bi mā akhfaytum wa mā āʿlantum wa may-yafʿalhu minkum faqad ḍalla sawā-a 's-sabīl.

In the Name of Allāh, Most Gracious, Most Merciful.

1. O you who have believed, do not take My enemies and your enemies as allies, extending to them affection while they have disbelieved in what came to you of the Truth, having driven out the Prophet and yourselves (only) because you believe in Allāh, your Lord. If you have come out for jihad in My Cause and seeking means to My Approval, (take them not as friends). You confide to them in affection, but I am most knowing of what you have concealed and what you have declared. And whoever does it among you has certainly strayed from the soundness of the Way.

(60:1)

سُورَةُ الصَّفِّ

61) Sūratu 'ṣ-Ṣāf, The Ranks

بِسْمِ اللهِ الرَّحْمٰنِ الرَّحِيمِ

سَبَّحَ لِلّٰهِ مَا فِى السَّمٰوَاتِ وَمَا فِى الْأَرْضِ

وَهُوَ الْعَزِيزُ الْحَكِيمُ ﴿١﴾

Bismillāhi 'r-Raḥmāni 'r-Raḥīm.

1. *Sabbaḥa lillāhi mā fi 's-samāwāti wa mā fi 'l-arḍi wa huwa 'l-ʿazīzu 'l-ḥakīm.*

In the Name of Allāh, Most Gracious, Most Merciful.

1. Whatever is in the Heavens and whatever is on the Earth exalts Allāh, and He is The Exalted in Might, The Wise.

(61:1)

۞

سُورَةُ الْجُمُعَةِ

62) Sūratu 'l-Jumu'ah, The Friday Congregation

بِسْمِ اللهِ الرَّحْمٰنِ الرَّحِيمِ

يُسَبِّحُ لِلّٰهِ مَا فِى السَّمٰوَاتِ وَمَا فِى الْأَرْضِ الْمَلِكِ الْقُدُّوسِ
الْعَزِيزِ الْحَكِيمِ ﴿١﴾

Bismillāhi 'r-Raḥmāni 'r-Raḥīm.

1. *Yusabbiḥu liLlāhi mā fi 's-samāwāti wa mā fi 'l-arḍi 'l-māliki 'l-quddūsi 'l-'azīzi 'l-ḥakīm.*

In the Name of Allāh, Most Gracious, Most Merciful.

1. Whatever is in the Heavens and whatever is on the Earth is exalting Allāh, The Sovereign, The Pure, The Exalted in Might, The Wise.

(62:1)

سُورَةُ الْمُنَافِقُونَ

63) Sūratu 'l-Munāfiqūn, The Hypocrites

بِسْمِ اللهِ الرَّحْمٰنِ الرَّحِيمِ

إِذَا جَاءَكَ الْمُنَافِقُونَ قَالُوا نَشْهَدُ إِنَّكَ لَرَسُولُ اللهِ وَاللهُ يَعْلَمُ
إِنَّكَ لَرَسُولُهُ وَاللهُ يَشْهَدُ إِنَّ الْمُنَافِقِينَ لَكَاذِبُونَ ﴿١﴾

Bismillāhi 'r-Raḥmāni 'r-Raḥīm.

1. *Idhā jā-aka 'l-munāfiqūna qālū nashhadu innaka la-rasūlullāhi wa 'Llāhu yaʿlamu innaka la-rasūluhu wa 'Llāhu yashhadu inna 'l-munāfiqīna la-kādhibūn.*

In the Name of Allāh, Most Gracious, Most Merciful.

1. When the hypocrites come to you, (O Muḥammad), they say, "We testify that you are the Messenger of Allāh." And Allāh knows that you are His Messenger, and Allāh testifies that the hypocrites are liars.

(63:1)

سُورَةُ التَّغَابُنِ

64) Sūratu 't-Taghābun, The Loss and Gain

بِسْمِ اللهِ الرَّحْمٰنِ الرَّحِيمِ

يُسَبِّحُ لِلّٰهِ مَا فِى السَّمٰوَاتِ وَمَا فِى الْاَرْضِۚ لَهُ الْمُلْكُ وَلَهُ
الْحَمْدُ وَهُوَ عَلٰى كُلِّ شَىْءٍ قَدِيرٌ ﴿١﴾

Bismillāhi 'r-Raḥmāni 'r-Raḥīm.

1. *Yusabbiḥu lillāhi mā fi 's-samāwāti wa mā fi 'l-arḍi lahu 'l-mulku wa lahu 'l-ḥamdu wa huwa ʿalā kulli shay-in qadīr.*

In the Name of Allāh, Most Gracious, Most Merciful.

1. Whatever is in the Heavens and whatever is on the Earth is exalting Allāh. To Him belongs dominion, and to Him belongs (all) praise, and He is over all things competent.

(64:1)

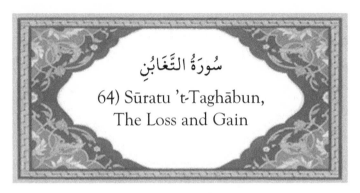

سُورَةُ الطَّلَاقِ

65) Sūratu 'ṭ-Ṭalāq, The Divorce

بِسْمِ اللهِ الرَّحْمٰنِ الرَّحِيمِ

يَا أَيُّهَا النَّبِيُّ إِذَا طَلَّقْتُمُ النِّسَاءَ فَطَلِّقُوهُنَّ لِعِدَّتِهِنَّ
وَأَحْصُوا الْعِدَّةَ وَاتَّقُوا اللهَ رَبَّكُمْ لَا تُخْرِجُوهُنَّ مِنْ بُيُوتِهِنَّ
وَلَا يَخْرُجْنَ إِلَّا أَنْ يَأْتِينَ بِفَاحِشَةٍ مُبَيِّنَةٍ وَتِلْكَ حُدُودُ اللهِ
وَمَنْ يَتَعَدَّ حُدُودَ اللهِ فَقَدْ ظَلَمَ نَفْسَهُ لَا تَدْرِي لَعَلَّ اللهَ
يُحْدِثُ بَعْدَ ذٰلِكَ أَمْرًا ﴿١﴾

Bismillāhi 'r-Raḥmāni 'r-Raḥīm.

1. *Yā ayyuha 'n-nabīyyu idhā ṭallaqtumu 'n-nisā-a fa ṭalliqūhunna li ʿiddatihinna wa aḥsu 'l-ʿiddata wattaqu 'Llāha rabbakum lā tukhrijūhunna min buyūtihinna wa lā yakhrujna illā an ya'tīna bi fāḥishatim-mubayyinatiwwa tilka ḥudūdu 'Llāhi wa man yataʿadda ḥudūda 'Llāhi faqad ẓalama*

nafsahu lā tadrī laʿalla 'Llāha yuḥdithu baʿada dhālika amrā.

In the Name of Allāh, Most Gracious, Most Merciful.

1. O Prophet, when you (Muslims) divorce women, divorce them for (the commencement of) their waiting period and keep count of the waiting period, and fear Allāh, your Lord. Do not turn them out of their (husbands') houses, nor should they (themselves) leave (during that period) unless they are committing a clear immorality. And those are the limits (set by) Allāh. And whoever transgresses the limits of Allāh has certainly wronged himself. You know not, perhaps Allāh will bring about after that a (different) matter.

(65:1)

سُورَةُ التَّحْرِيم

66) Sūratu 't-Taḥrīm, The Prohibition

بِسْمِ اللهِ الرَّحْمٰنِ الرَّحِيمِ

يَآ أَيُّهَا النَّبِيُّ لِمَ تُحَرِّمُ مَآ أَحَلَّ اللهُ لَكَ تَبْتَغِي مَرْضَاتَ
أَزْوَاجِكَ وَاللهُ غَفُورٌ رَحِيمٌ ﴿١﴾

Bismillāhi 'r-Raḥmāni 'r-Raḥīm.

1. *Yā ayyuha 'n-nabīyyu lima tuḥarrimu mā aḥalla 'Llāhu laka tabtaghī marḍāta azwājika wa 'Llāhu ghafūru 'r-raḥīm.*

In the Name of Allāh, Most Gracious, Most Merciful.

1. O Prophet, why do you prohibit (yourself from) what Allāh has made lawful for you, seeking the approval of your wives? And Allāh is Forgiving and Merciful.

(66:1)

❁

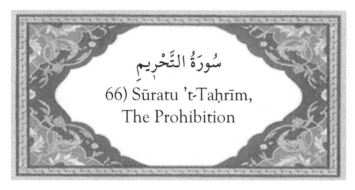

سُورَةُ الْمُلْكِ

67) Sūratu 'l-Mulk, The Dominion

بِسْمِ اللهِ الرَّحْمٰنِ الرَّحِيمِ

تَبَارَكَ الَّذِى بِيَدِهِ الْمُلْكُ وَهُوَ عَلٰى كُلِّ شَىْءٍ قَدِيرٌ ﴿١﴾

Bismillāhi 'r-Raḥmāni 'r-Raḥīm.

1. *Tabāraka 'Lladhī bi yadihi 'l-mulku wa huwa ʿalā kulli shay-in qadīr.*

In the Name of Allāh, Most Gracious, Most Merciful.

1. Blessed is He in Whose Hand is the Dominion, and He is over all things competent.

(67:1)

سُورَةُ الْقَلَمِ

68) Sūratu 'l-Qalam, The Pen

بِسْمِ اللهِ الرَّحْمٰنِ الرَّحِيمِ

نٓ وَالْقَلَمِ وَمَا يَسْطُرُونَ ﴿١﴾

Bismillāhi 'r-Raḥmāni 'r-Raḥīm.

1. *Nūn. Wa 'l-qalami wa mā yasṭurūn.*

In the Name of Allāh, Most Gracious, Most Merciful.

1. *Nūn*. By the Pen and what they inscribe.

(68:1)

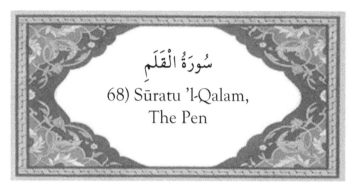

سُورَةُ الْقَلَمِ

69) Sūratu 'l-Ḥāqqah, The Inevitable Reality

بِسْمِ اللهِ الرَّحْمٰنِ الرَّحِيمِ

اَلْحَاقَّةُ ﴿١﴾ مَا الْحَاقَّةُ ﴿٢﴾ وَمَآ اَدْرٰيكَ مَا الْحَاقَّةُ ﴿٣﴾

Bismillāhi 'r-Raḥmāni 'r-Raḥīm.

1. *Al-ḥāqqah.*
2. *Ma 'l-ḥāqqah.*
3. *Wa mā adrāka ma 'l-ḥāqqah.*

In the Name of Allāh, Most Gracious, Most Merciful.

1. The Inevitable Reality.
2. What is the Inevitable Reality?
3. And what can make you know what is the Inevitable Reality?

(69:1-3)

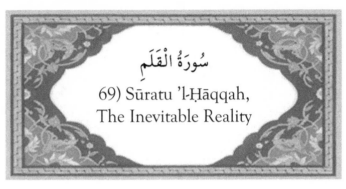

سُورَةُ الْمَعَارِجِ

70) Sūratu 'l-Ma'ārij, The Ascending Stairways

بِسْمِ اللهِ الرَّحْمٰنِ الرَّحِيمِ

سَأَلَ سَآئِلٌ بِعَذَابٍ وَاقِعٍ ﴿١﴾ لِّلْكَافِرِينَ لَيْسَ لَهُ دَافِعٌ ﴿٢﴾

Bismillāhi 'r-Raḥmāni 'r-Raḥīm.

1. *Sa'ala sā'ilum-bi 'adhābiw-wāqi'.*
2. *Li 'l-kāfirīna laysa lahu dāfi'.*

In the Name of Allāh, Most Gracious, Most Merciful.

1. A supplicant asked for a punishment bound to happen.
2. To the disbelievers, of it there is no preventer.

(70:1-2)

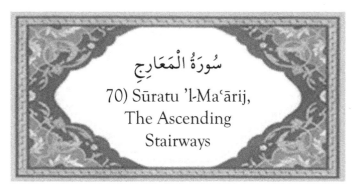

سُورَةُ نُوحٍ

71) Sūrat Nūḥ, Noah

بِسْمِ اللهِ الرَّحْمٰنِ الرَّحِيمِ

اِنَّآ اَرْسَلْنَا نُوحًا اِلٰى قَوْمِهٖٓ اَنْ اَنْذِرْ قَوْمَكَ مِنْ قَبْلِ اَنْ
يَأْتِيَهُمْ عَذَابٌ اَلِيمٌ ﴿١﴾

Bismillāhi 'r-Raḥmāni 'r-Raḥīm.

1. *Innā arsalnā nūḥan ilā qawmihī an andhir qawmaka min qabli ay-yā'tiyahum 'adhābun alīm.*

In the Name of Allāh, Most Gracious, Most Merciful.

1. Indeed, We sent Noah to his people, (saying), "Warn your people before there comes to them a painful punishment."

(71:1)

سُورَةُ الْجِنِّ

72) Sūratu 'l-Jinn, The Jinn

بِسْمِ اللهِ الرَّحْمٰنِ الرَّحِيمِ

قُلْ أُوحِيَ إِلَيَّ أَنَّهُ اسْتَمَعَ نَفَرٌ مِنَ الْجِنِّ فَقَالُوا إِنَّا سَمِعْنَا
قُرْآنًا عَجَبًا ﴿١﴾ يَهْدِي إِلَى الرُّشْدِ فَآمَنَّا بِهِ وَلَنْ نُشْرِكَ بِرَبِّنَا
أَحَدًا ﴿٢﴾

Bismillāhi 'r-Raḥmāni 'r-Raḥīm.

1. *Qul ūḥiya ilayya annahu 'stamaʿa nafarum-mina 'l-jinni fa qālū innā samiʿnā qur'ānan ʿajabā.*
2. *Yahdī ila 'r-rushdi fa āmannā bihi wa lan nushrika bi rabbinā aḥadā.*

In the Name of Allāh, Most Gracious, Most Merciful.

1. Say, (O Muḥammad), "It has been revealed to me that a group of the jinn listened and said, 'Indeed, we have heard an amazing Qur'an.

2. It guides to the right course, and we have believed in it. And we will never associate with our Lord anyone.'"

(72:1-2)

سُورَةُ الْمُزَّمِّلِ

73) Sūratu 'l-Muzzammil, The Enwrapped One

بِسْمِ اللّٰهِ الرَّحْمٰنِ الرَّحِيمِ

يَٓا اَيُّهَا الْمُزَّمِّلُۙ ﴿١﴾ قُمِ الَّيْلَ اِلَّا قَلِيلاًۙ ﴿٢﴾

نِصْفَهُٓ اَوِ انْقُصْ مِنْهُ قَلِيلاًۙ ﴿٣﴾

Bismillāhi 'r-Raḥmāni 'r-Raḥīm.

1. *Yā ayyuha 'l-muzzammil.*
2. *Qumi 'l-layla illā qalīlā.*
3. *Niṣfahu awi 'nquṣ minhu qalīlā.*

In the Name of Allāh, Most Gracious, Most Merciful.

1. O you who wraps himself (in clothing).
2. Arise (to pray) the night, except for a little.
3. Half of it, or subtract from it a little.

(73:1-3)

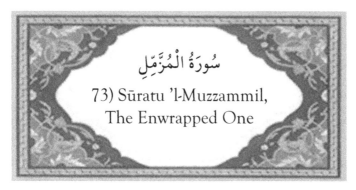

سُورَةُ الْمُدَّثِّرِ

74) Sūratu 'l-Muddaththir, The Cloaked One

بِسْمِ اللهِ الرَّحْمٰنِ الرَّحِيمِ

يَا اَيُّهَا الْمُدَّثِّرُ ﴿١﴾ قُمْ فَاَنْذِرْ ﴿٢﴾ وَرَبَّكَ فَكَبِّرْ ﴿٣﴾

Bismillāhi 'r-Raḥmāni 'r-Raḥīm.

1. *Yā ayyuha 'l-muddaththir.*
2. *Qum fa andhir.*
3. *Wa rabbaka fa kabbir.*

In the Name of Allāh, Most Gracious, Most Merciful.

1. O you who covers himself (with a garment).
2. Arise and warn.
3. And your Lord glorify.

(74:1-3)

سُورَةُ الْقِيٰمَةِ

75) Sūratu 'l-Qīyāmah, The Day of Resurrection

بِسْمِ اللهِ الرَّحْمٰنِ الرَّحِيمِ

لَآ أُقْسِمُ بِيَوْمِ الْقِيٰمَةِ ﴿١﴾ وَلَآ أُقْسِمُ بِالنَّفْسِ اللَّوَّامَةِ ﴿٢﴾

Bismillāhi 'r-Raḥmāni 'r-Raḥīm.

1. *Lā uqsimu bi yawmi 'l-qiyāmah.*
2. *Wa lā uqsimu bi 'n-nafsi 'l-lawwāmah.*

In the Name of Allāh, Most Gracious, Most Merciful.

1. I swear by the Day of Resurrection.
2. And I swear by the reproaching soul (to the certainty of resurrection).

(75:1-2)

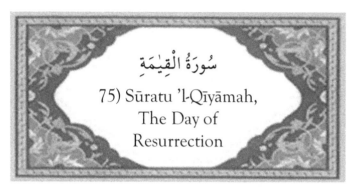

سُورَةُ الْاِنْسَانِ

76) Sūratu 'l-Insān, Humankind

بِسْمِ اللّٰهِ الرَّحْمٰنِ الرَّحِيمِ

هَلْ اَتٰى عَلَى الْاِنْسَانِ حِينٌ مِنَ الدَّهْرِ لَمْ يَكُنْ شَيْـًٔا
مَذْكُورًا ﴿١﴾

Bismillāhi 'r-Raḥmāni 'r-Raḥīm.

1. *Hal atā ʿalā 'l-insāni ḥīnum-mina 'd-dahri lam yakun shay-am-madhkūrā.*

In the Name of Allāh, Most Gracious, Most Merciful.

1. Has there (not) come upon Man a period of time when he was not a thing (even) mentioned?

(76:1)

سُورَةُ الْمُرْسَلَاتِ

77) Sūratu 'l-Murṣalāt, The Emissaries

بِسْمِ اللهِ الرَّحْمٰنِ الرَّحِيمِ

وَالْمُرْسَلَاتِ عُرْفًا ﴿١﴾ فَالْعَاصِفَاتِ عَصْفًا ﴿٢﴾

Bismillāhi 'r-Raḥmāni 'r-Raḥīm.

1. *Wa 'l-murṣalāti ʿurfā.*
2. *Fa-l-ʿāṣifāti ʿaṣfā.*

In the Name of Allāh, Most Gracious, Most Merciful.

1. By those (winds) sent forth in gusts.
2. And the winds that blow violently.

(77:1-2)

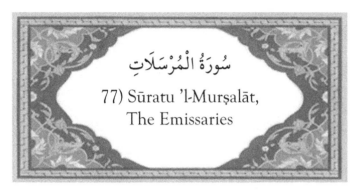

سُورَةُ النَّبَإِ

78) Sūratu 'n-Nabā', The Great News

بِسْمِ اللهِ الرَّحْمٰنِ الرَّحِيمِ

عَمَّ يَتَسَآءَلُونَ ﴿١﴾ عَنِ النَّبَإِ الْعَظِيمِ ﴿٢﴾

الَّذِى هُمْ فِيهِ مُخْتَلِفُونَ ﴿٣﴾

Bismillāhi 'r-Raḥmāni 'r-Raḥīm.

1. *'Amma yatasā'alūn.*
2. *'Ani 'n-naba-i 'l-'aẓīm.*
3. *Alladhī hum fīhi mukhtalifūn.*

In the Name of Allāh, Most Gracious, Most Merciful.

1. About what are they asking one another?
2. About the Great News.
3. That over which they are in disagreement.

(78:1-3)

سُورَةُ النَّازِعَاتِ

79) Sūratu 'n-Nāziʿāt, Those That Rise

بِسْمِ اللهِ الرَّحْمٰنِ الرَّحِيمِ

وَالنَّازِعَاتِ غَرْقًا ﴿١﴾ وَالنَّاشِطَاتِ نَشْطًا ﴿٢﴾

Bismillāhi 'r-Raḥmāni 'r-Raḥīm.

1. *Wa 'n-nāziʿāti gharqā.*
2. *Wa 'n-nāshiṭāti nashṭā.*

In the Name of Allāh, Most Gracious, Most Merciful.

1. By those (angels) who extract with violence
2. And (by) those who remove with ease.

(79:1-2)

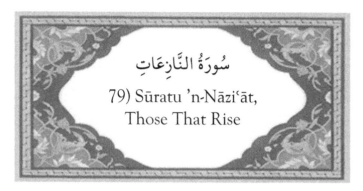

سُورَةُ عَبَسَ

80) Sūrat ʿAbasa, He Frowned

بِسْمِ اللهِ الرَّحْمٰنِ الرَّحِيمِ

عَبَسَ وَتَوَلّٰىٓ ﴿١﴾ اَنْ جَآءَهُ الْاَعْمٰىؕ ﴿٢﴾

Bismillāhi 'r-Raḥmāni 'r-Raḥīm.

1. *ʿAbasa wa tawallā.*
2. *An jā-ahu 'l-āʿmā.*

In the Name of Allāh, Most Gracious, Most Merciful.

1. He frowned and turned away.
2. Because there came unto him the blind man.

(80:1-2)

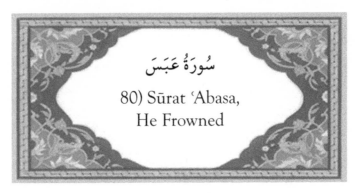

سُورَةُ التَّكْوِيرِ

81) Sūratu 't-Takwīr, The Folding Up

بِسْمِ اللهِ الرَّحْمٰنِ الرَّحِيمِ

إِذَا الشَّمْسُ كُوِّرَتْ ﴿١﴾ وَإِذَا النُّجُومُ انْكَدَرَتْ ﴿٢﴾

Bismillāhi 'r-Raḥmāni 'r-Raḥīm.

1. *Idhā 'sh-shamsu kuwwirat.*
2. *Wa idhā 'n-nujūmu 'n-kadarat.*

In the Name of Allāh, Most Gracious, Most Merciful.

1. When the sun is wrapped up (in darkness).
2. And when the stars fall, dispersing.

(81:1-2)

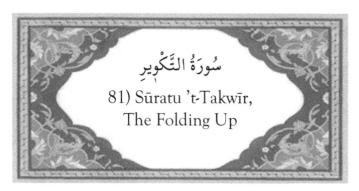

سُورَةُ الْانْفِطَارِ

82) Sūratu 'l-Infiṭār, The Cleaving Asunder

بِسْمِ اللهِ الرَّحْمٰنِ الرَّحِيمِ

إِذَا السَّمَاءُ انْفَطَرَتْ ﴿١﴾ وَإِذَا الْكَوَاكِبُ انْتَثَرَتْ ﴿٢﴾

Bismillāhi 'r-Raḥmāni 'r-Raḥīm.

1. *Idhā 's-samā'u 'n-faṭarat.*
2. *Wa idhā 'l-kawākibu 'n-tatharat.*

In the Name of Allāh, Most Gracious, Most Merciful.

1. When the sky breaks apart.
2. And when the stars fall, scattering.

(82:1-2)

سُورَةُ الْمُطَفِّفِينَ

83) Sūratu 'l-Muṭaffifīn, The Cheaters

بِسْمِ اللهِ الرَّحْمٰنِ الرَّحِيمِ

وَيْلٌ لِلْمُطَفِّفِينَ ﴿١﴾ اَلَّذِينَ اِذَا اكْتَالُوا عَلَى النَّاسِ
يَسْتَوْفُونَ ﴿٢﴾ وَاِذَا كَالُوهُمْ اَوْ وَزَنُوهُمْ يُخْسِرُونَ ﴿٣﴾

Bismillāhi 'r-Raḥmāni 'r-Raḥīm.

1. *Waylul li 'l-muṭaffifīn.*
2. *Alladhīna idha 'ktālū ʿala 'n-nāsi yastawfūn.*
3. *Wa idhā kālūhum aw wazanūhum yukhsirūn.*

In the Name of Allāh, Most Gracious, Most Merciful.

1. Woe to those who give less (than due).
2. Who, when they take a measure from people, take in full.
3. But if they give by measure or by weight to them, they cause loss.

(83:1-3)

سُورَةُ الْاِنْشِقَاقِ

84) Sūratu 'l-Inshiqāq, The Splitting Open

بِسْمِ اللهِ الرَّحْمٰنِ الرَّحِيمِ

إِذَا السَّمَآءُ انْشَقَّتْ ﴿١﴾ وَأَذِنَتْ لِرَبِّهَا وَحُقَّتْ ﴿٢﴾

Bismillāhi 'r-Raḥmāni 'r-Raḥīm.

1. *Idhā 's-samā'u 'n-shaqqat.*
2. *Wa adhinat li-rabbihā wa ḥuqqat.*

In the Name of Allāh, Most Gracious, Most Merciful.

1. When the sky has split (open).
2. And has responded to its Lord and was obligated (to do so).

(84:1-2)

❁

سُورَةُ الْبُرُوجِ

85) Sūratu 'l-Burūj, The Great Constellations

بِسْمِ اللهِ الرَّحْمٰنِ الرَّحِيمِ

وَالسَّمَآءِ ذَاتِ الْبُرُوجِ ﴿١﴾ وَالْيَوْمِ الْمَوْعُودِ ﴿٢﴾

وَشَاهِدٍ وَمَشْهُودٍ ﴿٣﴾

Bismillāhi 'r-Raḥmāni 'r-Raḥīm.

1. *Wa 's-samā-i dhāti 'l-burūj.*
2. *Wa 'l-yawmi 'l-maw'ūd.*
3. *Wa shāhidi 'w-wa mashhūd.*

In the Name of Allāh, Most Gracious, Most Merciful.

1. By the sky containing great stars.
2. And (by) the Promised Day.
3. And (by) the witness and what is witnessed.

(85:1-3)

سُورَةُ الطَّارِقِ

86) Sūratu 'ṭ-Ṭāriq, The Morning Star

بِسْمِ اللهِ الرَّحْمٰنِ الرَّحِيمِ

وَالسَّمَآءِ وَالطَّارِقِ ﴿١﴾ وَمَآ اَدْرٰيكَ مَا الطَّارِقُ ﴿٢﴾

اَلنَّجْمُ الثَّاقِبُ ﴿٣﴾

Bismillāhi 'r-Raḥmāni 'r-Raḥīm.

1. *Wa 's-samā-i wa 'ṭ-ṭāriq.*
2. *Wa mā adrāka mā 'ṭ-ṭāriq*
3. *An-najmu 'th-thāqib.*

In the Name of Allāh, Most Gracious, Most Merciful.

1. By the sky and the night comer.
2. And what can make you know what is the night comer?
3. It is the piercing star.

(86:1-3)

سُورَةُ الْأَعْلَىٰ

87) Sūratu 'l-Āʿlā, The Most High

بِسْمِ اللَّهِ الرَّحْمَٰنِ الرَّحِيمِ

سَبِّحِ اسْمَ رَبِّكَ الْأَعْلَى ﴿١﴾ الَّذِي خَلَقَ فَسَوَّىٰ ﴿٢﴾

Bismillāhi 'r-Raḥmāni 'r-Raḥīm.

1. *Sabbiḥi 'sma rabbika 'l-āʿlā.*
2. *Alladhī khalaqa fa-sawwā.*

In the Name of Allāh, Most Gracious, Most Merciful.

1. Exalt the Name of your Lord, The Most High,
2. Who created and proportioned.

(87:1-2)

سُورَةُ الْغَاشِيَةِ

88) Sūratu 'l-Ghāshīyah, The Overwhelming Event

بِسْمِ اللهِ الرَّحْمٰنِ الرَّحِيمِ

هَلْ أَتٰيكَ حَدِيثُ الْغَاشِيَةِ ﴿١﴾ وُجُوهٌ يَوْمَئِذٍ خَاشِعَةٌ ﴿٢﴾

Bismillāhi 'r-Raḥmāni 'r-Raḥīm.

1. *Hal atāka ḥadīthu 'l-ghāshīyah.*
2. *Wujūhuyyawma'idhin khāshiʿah.*

In the Name of Allāh, Most Gracious, Most Merciful.

1. Has there reached you the report of the Overwhelming Event?
2. (Some) faces, that Day, will be humbled.

(88:1-2)

سُورَةُ الْفَجْرِ

89) Sūratu 'l-Fajr, The Dawn

بِسْمِ اللهِ الرَّحْمٰنِ الرَّحِيمِ

وَالْفَجْرِ ﴿١﴾ وَلَيَالٍ عَشْرٍ ﴿٢﴾ وَالشَّفْعِ وَالْوَتْرِ ﴿٣﴾

وَالَّيْلِ إِذَا يَسْرِ ﴿٤﴾ هَلْ فِى ذٰلِكَ قَسَمٌ لِّذِى حِجْرٍ ﴿٥﴾

Bismillāhi 'r-Raḥmāni 'r-Raḥīm.

1. *Wa 'l-fajr.*
2. *Wa layālin ʿashr.*
3. *Wa 'sh-shafʿi wa 'l-watr.*
4. *Wa 'l-layli idhā yasr.*
5. *Hal fī dhālika qasamun lidhī ḥijr.*

In the Name of Allāh, Most Gracious, Most Merciful.

1. By the dawn.
2. And (by) ten nights.
3. And (by) the even (number) and the odd.
4. And (by) the night when it passes.

5. Is there (not) in (all) that an oath (sufficient) for one of perception?

(89:1-5)

سُورَةُ الْبَلَدِ

90) Sūratu 'l-Balad, The City

بِسْمِ اللهِ الرَّحْمٰنِ الرَّحِيمِ

لَآ أُقْسِمُ بِهٰذَا الْبَلَدِ ﴿١﴾ وَأَنْتَ حِلٌّۢ بِهٰذَا الْبَلَدِ ﴿٢﴾

Bismillāhi 'r-Raḥmāni 'r-Raḥīm.

1. *Lā uqsimu bi hādha 'l-balad.*
2. *Wa anta ḥillum bi hādha 'l-balad.*

In the Name of Allāh, Most Gracious, Most Merciful.

1. I swear by this city (Mecca).
2. And you, (O Muḥammad), are free of restriction in this city.

(90:1-2)

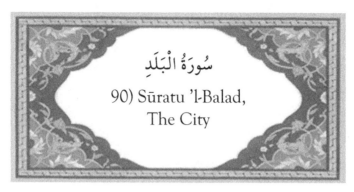

سُورَةُ الشَّمْسِ

91) Sūratu 'sh-Shams, The Sun

بِسْمِ اللهِ الرَّحْمٰنِ الرَّحِيمِ

وَالشَّمْسِ وَضُحٰيهَا ﴿١﴾ وَالْقَمَرِ اِذَا تَلٰيهَا ﴿٢﴾

Bismillāhi 'r-Raḥmāni 'r-Raḥīm.

1. *Wa 'sh-shamsi wa duḥāhā.*
2. *Wa 'l-qamari idhā talāhā.*

In the Name of Allāh, Most Gracious, Most Merciful.

1. By the sun and its brightness.
2. And (by) the moon when it follows it.

(91:1-2)

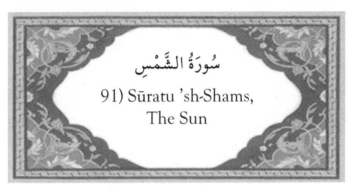

سُورَةُ اللَّيْلِ

92) Sūratu 'l-Layl, The Night

بِسْمِ اللَّهِ الرَّحْمَٰنِ الرَّحِيمِ

وَاللَّيْلِ إِذَا يَغْشَىٰ ﴿١﴾ وَالنَّهَارِ إِذَا تَجَلَّىٰ ﴿٢﴾

Bismillāhi 'r-Raḥmāni 'r-Raḥīm.

1. *Wa 'l-layli idhā yaghshā.*
2. *Wa 'n-nahāri idhā tajallā.*

In the Name of Allāh, Most Gracious, Most Merciful.

1. By the night when it covers.
2. And (by) the day when it appears.

(92:1-2)

سُورَةُ الضُّحَىٰ

93) Sūrat aḍ-Ḍuhā, The Glorious Morning Light

بِسْمِ اللَّهِ الرَّحْمَٰنِ الرَّحِيمِ

وَالضُّحَىٰ ﴿١﴾ وَاللَّيْلِ إِذَا سَجَىٰ ﴿٢﴾

مَا وَدَّعَكَ رَبُّكَ وَمَا قَلَىٰ ﴿٣﴾

Bismillāhi 'r-Raḥmāni 'r-Raḥīm.

1. *Wa 'ḍ-ḍuḥā.*
2. *Wa 'l-layli idhā sajā.*
3. *Mā wadda'aka rabbuka wa mā qalā.*

In the Name of Allāh, Most Gracious, Most Merciful.

1. By the morning brightness.
2. And (by) the night when it covers with darkness.
3. Your Lord has not taken leave of you, (O Muḥammad), nor has He detested (you).

(93:1-3)

✡

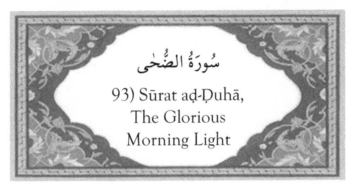

سُورَةُ الْاِنْشِرَاحِ

94) Sūratu 'l-Inshirāḥ, The Expansion of the Chest

بِسْمِ اللهِ الرَّحْمٰنِ الرَّحِيمِ

اَلَمْ نَشْرَحْ لَكَ صَدْرَكَ ﴿١﴾ وَوَضَعْنَا عَنْكَ وِزْرَكَ ﴿٢﴾

Bismillāhi 'r-Raḥmāni 'r-Raḥīm.

1. *Alam nashraḥ laka ṣadrak.*
2. *Wa waḍaʿna ʿanka wizrak.*

In the Name of Allāh, Most Gracious, Most Merciful.

1. Did We not expand for you, (O Muḥammad), your chest?
2. And We removed from you your burden.

(94:1-2)

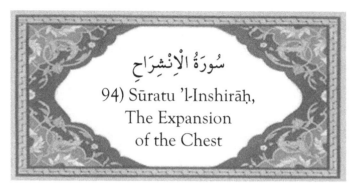

سُورَةُ التِّينِ

95) Sūratu 't-Tīn, The Fig

بِسْمِ اللهِ الرَّحْمٰنِ الرَّحِيمِ

وَالتِّينِ وَالزَّيْتُونِ ﴿١﴾ وَطُورِ سِينِينَ ﴿٢﴾

Bismillāhi 'r-Raḥmāni 'r-Raḥīm.

1. *Wa 't-tīni wa 'z-zaytūn.*
2. *Wa ṭūri sīnīn.*

In the Name of Allāh, Most Gracious, Most Merciful.

1. By the fig and the olive.
2. And (by) Mount Sinai.

(95:1-2)

سُورَةُ الْعَلَقِ

96) Sūratu 'l-'Alaq, The Clinging Clot

بِسْمِ اللهِ الرَّحْمٰنِ الرَّحِيمِ

اِقْرَأْ بِاسْمِ رَبِّكَ الَّذِى خَلَقَ ﴿١﴾ خَلَقَ الْاِنْسَانَ مِنْ عَلَقٍ ﴿٢﴾

Bismillāhi 'r-Raḥmāni 'r-Raḥīm.

1. *Iqrā' bismi rabbika 'Lladhī khalaq.*
2. *Khalaqa 'l-insāna min 'alaq.*

In the Name of Allāh, Most Gracious, Most Merciful.

1. Recite in the Name of your Lord Who created.
2. Created Man from a clinging substance.

(96:1-2)

سُورَةُ الْقَدْرِ

97) Sūratu 'l-Qadr, The Night of Honor

بِسْمِ اللهِ الرَّحْمٰنِ الرَّحِيمِ

إِنَّآ اَنْزَلْنَاهُ فِى لَيْلَةِ الْقَدْرِ ﴿١﴾ وَمَآ اَدْرٰيكَ مَا لَيْلَةُ
الْقَدْرِ ﴿٢﴾

Bismillāhi 'r-Raḥmāni 'r-Raḥīm.

1. *Innā anzalnāhu fī laylati 'l-qadr.*
2. *Wa mā adrāka mā laylatu 'l-qadr.*

In the Name of Allāh, Most Gracious, Most Merciful.

1. Indeed, We sent the Qur'an down during the Night of Power.
2. And what can make you know what is the Night of Power?

(97:1-2)

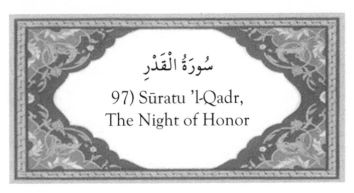

سُورَةُ الْبَيِّنَةِ

98) Sūratu 'l-Bayyinah, The Clear Evidence

بِسْمِ اللهِ الرَّحْمٰنِ الرَّحِيمِ

لَمْ يَكُنِ الَّذِينَ كَفَرُوا مِنْ اَهْلِ الْكِتَابِ وَالْمُشْرِكِينَ
مُنْفَكِّينَ حَتّٰى تَأْتِيَهُمُ الْبَيِّنَةُ ﴿١﴾

Bismillāhi 'r-Raḥmāni 'r-Raḥīm.

1. *Lam yakuni 'Lladhīna kafarū min āhli 'l-kitābi wa 'l-mushrikīna munfakkīna ḥattā tā'tiyahumu 'l-bayyinah.*

In the Name of Allāh, Most Gracious, Most Merciful.

1. Those who disbelieved among the People of the Scripture and the polytheists were not to be parted (from misbelief) until there came to them clear evidence.

(98:1)

سُورَةُ الزَّلْزَلَة

99) Sūratu 'z-Zalzalah, The Earthquake

بِسْمِ اللّٰهِ الرَّحْمٰنِ الرَّحِيمِ

إِذَا زُلْزِلَتِ الْأَرْضُ زِلْزَالَهَا ﴿١﴾ وَأَخْرَجَتِ الْأَرْضُ
أَثْقَالَهَا ﴿٢﴾

Bismillāhi 'r-Raḥmāni 'r-Raḥīm.

1. *Idhā zulzilati 'l-arḍu zilzālahā.*
2. *Wa akhrajati 'l-arḍu athqālahā.*

In the Name of Allāh, Most Gracious, Most Merciful.

1. When the Earth is shaken with its (final) earthquake.
2. And the Earth discharges its burdens.

(99:1-2)

۞

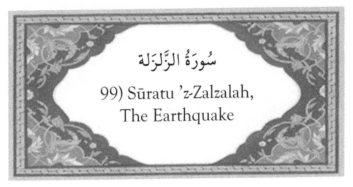

سُورَةُ الْعَادِيَاتِ

100) Sūratu 'l-'Adīyāt, The Racers

بِسْمِ اللهِ الرَّحْمٰنِ الرَّحِيمِ

وَالْعَادِيَاتِ ضَبْحاً ﴿١﴾ فَالْمُورِيَاتِ قَدْحاً ﴿٢﴾

Bismillāhi 'r-Raḥmāni 'r-Raḥīm.

1. *Wa 'l-'ādīyāti ḍabḥā.*
2. *Fa 'l-mūrīyāti qad-ḥā.*

In the Name of Allāh, Most Gracious, Most Merciful.

1. By the racers, panting.
2. And the producers of sparks (when) striking

(100:1-2)

سُورَةُ الْقَارِعَةِ

101) Sūratu 'l-Qāriʿah, The Striking Hour

بِسْمِ اللّٰهِ الرَّحْمٰنِ الرَّحِيمِ

اَلْقَارِعَةُ ﴿١﴾ مَا الْقَارِعَةُ ﴿٢﴾ وَمَآ اَدْرٰيكَ مَا الْقَارِعَةُ ﴿٣﴾

Bismillāhi 'r-Raḥmāni 'r-Raḥīm.

1. *Al-qāriʿah.*
2. *Mā 'l-qāriʿah.*
3. *Wa mā adrāka mā 'l-qāriʿah.*

In the Name of Allāh, Most Gracious, Most Merciful.

1. The Striking Calamity.
2. What is the Striking Calamity?
3. And what can make you know what is the Striking Calamity?

(101:1-3)

سُورَةُ التَّكَاثُرِ

102) Sūratu 't-Takāthur, The Piling Up

بِسْمِ اللهِ الرَّحْمٰنِ الرَّحِيمِ

اَلْهٰكُمُ التَّكَاثُرُ ﴿١﴾ حَتّٰى زُرْتُمُ الْمَقَابِرَ ﴿٢﴾

Bismillāhi 'r-Raḥmāni 'r-Raḥīm.

1. *Al-hākumu 't-takāthur.*
2. *Ḥattā zurtumu 'l-maqābir.*

In the Name of Allāh, Most Gracious, Most Merciful.

1. Competition in (worldly) increase diverts you.
2. Until you visit the graveyards.

(102:1-2)

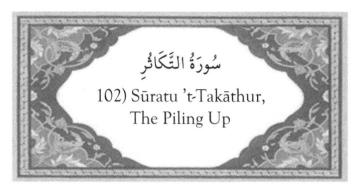

سُورَةُ الْعَصْرِ

103) Sūratu 'l-'Aṣr, The Time

بِسْمِ اللهِ الرَّحْمٰنِ الرَّحِيمِ

وَالْعَصْرِ ﴿١﴾ اِنَّ الْاِنْسَانَ لَفِى خُسْرٍ ﴿٢﴾

Bismillāhi 'r-Raḥmāni 'r-Raḥīm.

1. *Wa 'l-'aṣr.*
2. *Inna 'l-insāna la-fī khusr.*

In the Name of Allāh, Most Gracious, Most Merciful.

1. By Time.
2. Indeed, Mankind is in loss.

(103:1-2)

سُورَةُ الْهُمَزَةِ

104) Sūratu 'l-Humazah, The Slanderer

بِسْمِ اللهِ الرَّحْمٰنِ الرَّحِيمِ

وَيْلٌ لِكُلِّ هُمَزَةٍ لُمَزَةٍ ﴿١﴾ اَلَّذِى جَمَعَ مَالًا وَعَدَّدَهُ ﴿٢﴾

Bismillāhi 'r-Raḥmāni 'r-Raḥīm.

1. *Waylul li kulli humazati 'l-lumazah.*
2. *Alladhī jamaʿa mā law wa ʿaddadah.*

In the Name of Allāh, Most Gracious, Most Merciful.

1. Woe to every scorner and mocker.
2. Who collects wealth and (continuously) counts it.

(104:1-2)

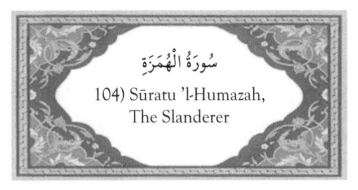

سُورَةُ الْفِيلِ

105) Sūratu 'l-Fīl, The Elephant

بِسْمِ اللهِ الرَّحْمٰنِ الرَّحِيمِ

اَلَمْ تَرَ كَيْفَ فَعَلَ رَبُّكَ بِاَصْحَابِ الْفِيلِ ﴿١﴾

Bismillāhi 'r-Raḥmāni 'r-Raḥīm.

1. *Alam tara kayfa faʿala rabbuka bi aṣ-ḥābi 'l-fīl.*

In the Name of Allāh, Most Gracious, Most Merciful.

1. Have you not considered, (O Muḥammad), how your Lord dealt with the companions of the elephant?

(105:1)

❁

سُورَةُ قُرَيْشٍ

106) Sūrat Quraysh, The Quraysh

بِسْمِ اللهِ الرَّحْمٰنِ الرَّحِيمِ

لِإِيلَافِ قُرَيْشٍ ﴿١﴾ إِيلَافِهِمْ رِحْلَةَ الشِّتَاءِ وَالصَّيْفِ ﴿٢﴾

Bismillāhi 'r-Raḥmāni 'r-Raḥīm.

1. *Li īlāfi quraysh.*
2. *Īlāfihim riḥlatā 'sh-shitā'i wa 'ṣ-ṣayf.*

In the Name of Allāh, Most Gracious, Most Merciful.

1. For the accustomed security of the Quraysh.
2. Their accustomed security (in) the caravan of winter and summer.

(106:1-2)

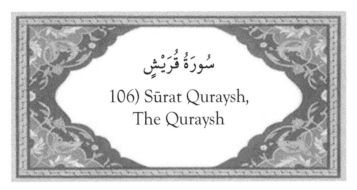

سُورَةُ الْمَاعُونِ

107) Sūratu 'l-Māʿūn, The Neighborly Assistance

بِسْمِ اللّٰهِ الرَّحْمٰنِ الرَّحِيمِ

اَرَاَيْتَ الَّذٖى يُكَذِّبُ بِالدّٖينِۜ ﴿١﴾ فَذٰلِكَ الَّذٖى يَدُعُّ الْيَتٖيمَۙ ﴿٢﴾

وَلَا يَحُضُّ عَلٰى طَعَامِ الْمِسْكٖينِۜ ﴿٣﴾

Bismillāhi 'r-Raḥmāni 'r-Raḥīm.

1. *Ara-ayta 'Lladhī yukadhdhibu bi 'd-dīn.*
2. *Fa dhālika 'Lladhī yaduʿul-yatīm*
3. *Wa lā yaḥuḍḍu ʿalā ṭaʿāmi 'l-miskīn.*

In the Name of Allāh, Most Gracious, Most Merciful.

1. Have you seen the one who denies the Recompense?
2. For that is the one who drives away the orphan.
3. And does not encourage the feeding of the poor.

(107:1-3)

سُورَةُ الْكَوْثَرِ

108) Sūratu 'l-Kawthar, The Abundance

بِسْمِ اللّٰهِ الرَّحْمٰنِ الرَّحِيمِ

إِنَّا أَعْطَيْنَاكَ الْكَوْثَرَ ﴿١﴾ فَصَلِّ لِرَبِّكَ وَانْحَرْ ﴿٢﴾

Bismillāhi 'r-Raḥmāni 'r-Raḥīm.

1. *Innā aʿṭaynāka 'l-kawthar.*
2. *Fa ṣalli li-rabbika wa 'nḥar.*

In the Name of Allāh, Most Gracious, Most Merciful.

1. Indeed, We have granted you, (O Muḥammad), al-Kawthar, the Fount (of Abundance).
2. So, pray to your Lord and sacrifice (to Him alone).

(108:1-2)

سُورَةُ الْكَافِرُونَ

109) Sūratu 'l-Kāfirūn, The Disbelievers

بِسْمِ اللهِ الرَّحْمٰنِ الرَّحِيمِ

قُلْ يَٓا اَيُّهَا الْكَافِرُونَۙ ﴿١﴾ لَٓا اَعْبُدُ مَا تَعْبُدُونَۙ ﴿٢﴾

وَلَٓا اَنْتُمْ عَابِدُونَ مَٓا اَعْبُدُۚ ﴿٣﴾

Bismillāhi 'r-Raḥmāni 'r-Raḥīm.

1. *Qul yā ayyuha 'l-kāfirūn.*
2. *Lā aʿbudu mā taʿbudūn.*
3. *Wa lā antum ʿābidūna mā āʿbud.*

In the Name of Allāh, Most Gracious, Most Merciful.

1. Say, "O Disbelievers!
2. I do not worship what you worship.
3. Nor are you worshippers of what I worship."

(109:1-3)

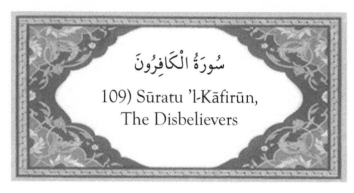

سُورَةُ النَّصْرِ

110) Sūratu 'n-Naṣr, The Victory

بِسْمِ اللهِ الرَّحْمٰنِ الرَّحِيمِ

إِذَا جَاءَ نَصْرُ اللهِ وَالْفَتْحُ ﴿١﴾

وَرَأَيْتَ النَّاسَ يَدْخُلُونَ فِي دِينِ اللهِ أَفْوَاجًا ﴿٢﴾

Bismillāhi 'r-Raḥmāni 'r-Raḥīm.

1. *Idhā jā'a naṣru 'Llāhi wa 'l-fatḥ.*
2. *Wa ra-ayta 'n-nāsa yadkhulūna fī dīni 'Llāhi afwājā.*

In the Name of Allāh, Most Gracious, Most Merciful.

1. When the victory of Allāh has come and the conquest.
2. And you see the people entering into the religion of Allāh in multitudes.

(110:1-2)

سُورَةُ الْمَسَدِ

111) Sūratu 'l-Masad, The Plaited Rope

بِسْمِ اللهِ الرَّحْمٰنِ الرَّحِيمِ

تَبَّتْ يَدَآ اَبِى لَهَبٍ وَتَبَّ ﴿١﴾ مَآ اَغْنٰى عَنْهُ مَالُهُ وَمَا
كَسَبَ ﴿٢﴾

Bismillāhi 'r-Raḥmāni 'r-Raḥīm.

1. *Tabbat yadā abī lahabi 'w-wa tabb.*
2. *Mā aghnā ʿanhu māluhu wa mā kasab.*

In the Name of Allāh, Most Gracious, Most Merciful.

1. May the hands of Abū Lahab be ruined, and ruined is he.
2. His wealth will not avail him or that which he gained.

(111:1-2)

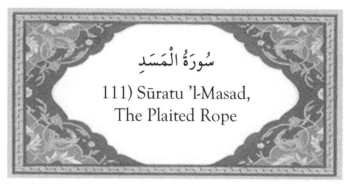

سُورَةُ الإِخْلَاصِ

112) Sūratu 'l-Ikhlāṣ, The Purity of Faith

بِسْمِ اللهِ الرَّحْمٰنِ الرَّحِيمِ

قُلْ هُوَ اللهُ اَحَدٌ ﴿١﴾ اَللهُ الصَّمَدُ ﴿٢﴾ لَمْ يَلِدْ وَلَمْ يُولَدْ ﴿٣﴾

وَلَمْ يَكُنْ لَهُ كُفُوًا اَحَدٌ ﴿٤﴾

Bismillāhi 'r-Raḥmāni 'r-Raḥīm.

1. *Qul hūwa 'Llāhu Āḥad.*
2. *Allāhu 'ṣ-Ṣamad.*
3. *Lam yalid wa lam yūlad.*
4. *Wa lam yaku 'l-lahu kufūwan āḥad.*

In the Name of Allāh, Most Gracious, Most Merciful.

1. Say, "He is Allāh, (Who is) One.
2. Allāh, the Eternal Refuge.
3. He neither begets nor is born.
4. Nor is there to Him any equivalent."

(112:1-4)

سُورَةُ الْفَلَقِ

113) Sūratu 'l-Falaq, The Daybreak

بِسْمِ اللهِ الرَّحْمٰنِ الرَّحِيمِ

قُلْ اَعُوذُ بِرَبِّ الْفَلَقِۙ ﴿١﴾ مِنْ شَرِّ مَا خَلَقَۙ ﴿٢﴾

وَمِنْ شَرِّ غَاسِقٍ اِذَا وَقَبَۙ ﴿٣﴾ وَمِنْ شَرِّ النَّفَّاثَاتِ فِى الْعُقَدِۙ ﴿٤﴾

وَمِنْ شَرِّ حَاسِدٍ اِذَا حَسَدَ ﴿٥﴾

Bismillāhi 'r-Raḥmāni 'r-Raḥīm.

1. *Qul aʿūdhu bi rabbi 'l-falaq.*
2. *Min sharri mā khalaq.*
3. *Wa min sharri ghāsiqin idhā waqab.*
4. *Wa min sharrin naffāthāti fi 'l-ʿuqad.*
5. *Wa min sharri ḥāsidin idhā ḥasad.*

In the Name of Allāh, Most Gracious, Most Merciful.

1. Say, "I seek refuge in the Lord of daybreak.
2. From the evil of that which He created.

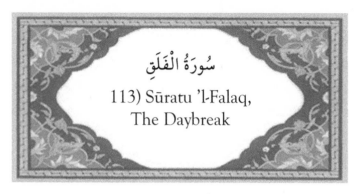

3. And from the evil of darkness when it settles.
4. And from the evil of the blowers in knots.
5. And from the evil of an envier when he envies."

(113:1-5)

سُورَةُ النَّاسِ

114) Sūratu 'n-Nās, Mankind

بِسْمِ اللهِ الرَّحْمٰنِ الرَّحِيمِ

قُلْ اَعُوذُ بِرَبِّ النَّاسِۙ ﴿١﴾ مَلِكِ النَّاسِۙ ﴿٢﴾

اِلٰهِ النَّاسِۙ ﴿٣﴾ مِنْ شَرِّ الْوَسْوَاسِ الْخَنَّاسِۙ ﴿٤﴾

اَلَّذٖى يُوَسْوِسُ فٖى صُدُورِ النَّاسِۙ ﴿٥﴾ مِنَ الْجِنَّةِ وَالنَّاسِ ﴿٦﴾

Bismillāhi 'r-Raḥmāni 'r-Raḥīm.

1. *Qul aʿūdhu bi rabbi 'n-nās.*
2. *Maliki 'n-nās.*
3. *Ilāhi 'n-nās.*
4. *Min sharri 'l-waswāsi 'l-khannās.*
5. *Alladhī yuwaswisu fī ṣudūri 'n-nās.*
6. *Mina 'l-jinnati wa 'n-nās.*

In the Name of Allāh, Most Gracious, Most Merciful.

1. Say, "I seek refuge in the Lord of Mankind,
2. The Sovereign of Mankind.

3. The God of Mankind,
4. From the evil of the retreating whisperer.
5. Who whispers (evil) into the breasts of Mankind.
6. From among the jinn and Mankind."

(114:1-6)

وَبَلَّغَ نَبِيّهُ الْكَرِيمَ وَنَحْنُ عَلَى ذَلِكَ مِنَ الشَّاهِدِينَ
الشَّاكِرِينَ بِقَلْبٍ سَلِيمٍ. سُبْحَانَ رَبِّكَ رَبِّ الْعِزَّةِ عَمَّا
يَصِفُونَ وَسَلَامٌ عَلَى الْمُرْسَلِينَ وَالْحَمْدُ لِلَّهِ رَبِّ الْعَالَمِينَ.
رَبَّنَا تَقَبَّلْ مِنَّا بِحُرْمَةِ مَنْ أَنْزَلْتَ عَلَيْهِ سِرِّ سُورَةِ الْفَاتِحَة.

Wa ballagha nabīyyuhu 'l-karīma wa naḥnu ʿalā dhālika min ash-shāhidīna 'sh-shākirīn bi qalbin salīm. Subḥāna rabbika rabbi 'l-ʿizzati ʿammā yasifūna wa salāmun ʿalā 'l-mursalīna wa 'l-ḥamduli 'Llāhi rabbi 'l-ʿālamīn. Rabbanā taqabbal minnā bi ḥurmati man anzalta ʿalayhi sirri sūrati 'l-Fātiḥa.

And His Noble Prophet truly conveyed the Message and we attest to that with gratitude and a sound heart. May Our Lord the Lord of Majesty be exalted above all descriptions, and peace be upon the Messengers and all praise for Allāh, the Lord of the Worlds. Our Lord, accept from us by the sanctity of the one to whom You revealed the secret of *Sūratu 'l-Fātiḥa*:

بِسْمِ اللهِ الرَّحْمٰنِ الرَّحِيمِ ﴿١﴾
اَلْحَمْدُ لِلّٰهِ رَبِّ الْعَالَمِينَۙ ﴿٢﴾ اَلرَّحْمٰنِ الرَّحِيمِۙ ﴿٣﴾
مَالِكِ يَوْمِ الدِّينِۜ ﴿٤﴾ اِيَّاكَ نَعْبُدُ وَاِيَّاكَ نَسْتَعِينُۜ ﴿٥﴾
اِهْدِنَا الصِّرَاطَ الْمُسْتَقِيمَۙ ﴿٦﴾

صِرَاطَ الَّذِينَ أَنْعَمْتَ عَلَيْهِمْ غَيْرِ الْمَغْضُوبِ عَلَيْهِمْ وَلَا الضَّالِّينَ ﴿٧﴾

Bismillāhi 'r-Raḥmāni 'r-Raḥīm.

AlḥamduliLlāhi Rabbi 'l-ʿAlamīn, ar-Raḥmāni 'r-Raḥīm, māliki yawmi 'd-dīn, īyyāka naʿbudu wa īyyāka nastaʿīn, ihdina ' ṣ-ṣirāṭa 'l-mustaqīm, ṣirāṭa 'Lladhīna anʿamta ʿalayhim, ghayri 'l-maghḍūbi ʿalayhim, wa la 'ḍ-ḍāllīn. Āmīn.

In the Name of Allāh, Most Gracious, Most Merciful. All Praise is due to Allāh alone, the Sustainer of all the Worlds, the Most Gracious, the Dispenser of Grace, Lord of the Day of Judgment! You Alone do we worship, and to You alone we return! Guide us to the Straight Way, the way of those upon whom You have bestowed Your Blessings, not of those who have been condemned (by You), nor of those who go astray.

Ameen.

(Sūratu 'l-Fātiḥa, 1:7)

سُورَةُ الْفَاتِحَةِ

1) Sūratu 'l-Fātiḥa
The Opening

بِسْمِ اللهِ الرَّحْمٰنِ الرَّحِيمِ ﴿١﴾

اَلْحَمْدُ لِلّٰهِ رَبِّ الْعَالَمِينَۙ ﴿٢﴾ اَلرَّحْمٰنِ الرَّحِيمِۙ ﴿٣﴾

مَالِكِ يَوْمِ الدِّينِۜ ﴿٤﴾

1. *Bismillāhi 'r-Raḥmāni 'r-Raḥīm.*
2. *Alḥamdulillāhi Rabbi 'l-'Alamīn.*
3. *Ar-Raḥmāni 'r-Raḥīm.*
4. *Māliki yawmi 'd-dīn.*

1. In the Name of Allāh, Most Gracious, Most Merciful.
2. All praise is due to Allāh, Lord of the Worlds.
3. Most Gracious, Most Merciful.
4. The Sovereign of the Day of Judgement.

(1:1-4)

سُورَةُ الْبَقَرَةِ

2) Sūratu 'l-Baqarah
The Cow

بِسْمِ اللهِ الرَّحْمٰنِ الرَّحِيمِ

الٓمٓ ﴿١﴾ ذٰلِكَ الْكِتَابُ لَا رَيْبَ فِيهِ هُدًى لِلْمُتَّقِينَ ﴿٢﴾

Bismillāhi 'r-Raḥmāni 'r-Raḥīm.

1. *Alif. Lām. Mīm.*
2. *Dhālika 'l-kitābu lā rayba fīhi huda 'l-li 'l-muttaqīn.*

In the Name of Allāh, Most Gracious, Most Merciful.

1. *Alif. Lām. Mīm.*
2. This is the Book about which there is no doubt, a guidance for those conscious of Allāh.

(2:1-2)

دعاء ختم القراءن

Duʿā Khatm al-Qur'an

Invocation for Completing the Qur'an

This *duʿā*, supplication, during which 70,000 angels descend to say "*Āmīn*," can be recited at every completion of the Holy Qur'an for any intention:

أعوذ بالله من الشيطان الرجيم

بسم الله الرحمن الرحيم

اللَّهُمَّ أرْحَمْنِى بِالْقُرْءَانً وَاجْعَلْهُ لِى إمَامًا وَنُورًا وَهُدًى وَرَحْمَة.

اللَّهُمَّ ذَكِّرْنِى مِنْهُ مَا نَسِيتُ وَعَلِّمْنِى مِنْهُ مَا جَهِلْتُ وَارْزُقْنِى تِلَاوَتَهُ

آنَاءَ اللَّيْلِ وَأَطْرَافَ النَّهَارِ وَأجْعَلْهُ لِى حُجَّةً يَارَبَّ الْعَالَمِينْ

Aʿūdhu billāhi mina 'sh-Shaytāni 'r-rajīm.

Bismillāhi 'r-Raḥmāni 'r-Raḥīm. Allāhumma arḥamnī bi 'l-qur'ānan w 'ajʿalhu lī imāman wa nūran wa hudan wa raḥmah. Allāhumma dhakkirnī minhu mā nasītu wa ʿallimnī minhu mā jahiltu w 'arzuqnī tilāwatahu anā al-layli wa aṭrāfa 'n-nahāri w 'ajʿalhu lī ḥujjatan yā Rabba 'l-ʿālamīn!

I seek refuge in Allāh from the accursed Shayṭān.

In the Name of Allāh, Most Gracious, Most Merciful.

O Allāh! Have mercy upon me through the Qur'an and make it for me a Guide, Light, Guidance and Mercy. O Allāh! Remind me of it what I have forgotten and teach me of it what I am ignorant of. Grant me to recite it in the depths of night and corners of the day and make it for me a proof, O Lord of the Worlds!

اللَّهُمَّ أَصْلِحْ لِي دِينِي الَّذِي هُوَ عِصْمَةُ أَمْرِي وَأَصْلِحْ لِي دُنْيَايَ الَّتِي فِيهَا مَعَاشِي وَأَصْلِحْ لِي آخِرَتِي الَّتِي فِيهَا مَعَادِي وَأَجْعَلُ الْحَيَاةَ زِيَادَةً لِي فِي كُلِّ خَيْرٍ وَأجْعَلُ الْمَوْتَ رَاحَةً لِي مِنْ كُلِّ شَرّْ

Allāhumma aṣliḥ lī dīni 'Lladhī hūwa ʿiṣmatu amrī wa aṣliḥ lī dunyāya allatī fīhā maʿāshīyy wa aṣliḥ lī ākhiratī allatī fīhā maʿādī w 'ajʿalu 'l-ḥayāta ziyādatan lī fī kulli khayrin w 'ajʿal al-mawta rāḥatan lī min kulli sharr.

O Allāh, make me adhere properly to my religion, on which all my affairs depend; make this world good for me in which is my livelihood; make my Hereafter good for me, in which is my ultimate destiny; make my life increase in every good thing and make my death a respite from every evil.

اللَّهُمَّ أجْعَلْ خَيْرَ عُمُرِى آخِرَهُ وَخَيْرَ عَمَلِى خَوَاتِمَهُ وَخَيْرَ أَيَّامِى يَوْمَ أَلْقَاكَ فِيه .اللَّهُمَّ إِنِّى أَسْأَلُكَ عِيْشَةً هَنِيَّةً وَمَيْتَةً سَوِيَّةً وَمَرَدًّا غَيْرَ مُخْزٍ وَلافَاضِحْ

Allāhumma 'j'al khayra 'umurī ākhirahu wa khayra 'amalī khawātimahu wa khayra ayyāmi yawma alqāka fīh. Allāhumma innī as'aluka 'īshatan hanīyyatan wa maytatan sawīyyatan wa maraddan ghayra mukhzin wa lā fāḍih.

O Allāh! Help better the last part of my life and the end of my deed, and may it be the best of my days when I meet You! O Allāh! I ask you for a clean life, a blissful death, and a return (to You) which is neither humiliating nor disgracing.

اللَّهُمَّ إِنِّى أَسْأَلُكَ خَيْرَ الْمَسْأَلَةِ وَخَيْرِ الدُّعَاءِ وَخَيْرَ النُّجَّاحِ وَخَيْرَ الْعِلْمِ وَخَيْرِالْعَمَلِ وَخَيْرَ الثَّوَابِ وَخَيْرَ الْحَيَاةِ وَخَيْرَالْمَمَاتِ وَثَبِّتْنِى وَثَقِّلْ مَوَازِينى وَحَقِّقْ إيمَانِى وَأرْفَعْ دَرَجَاتِى وَتَقَبَّلْ صَلاَتِى وَأغْفِر لِى خَطِيئَاتِى وَأَسْأَلُكَ الْعُلاَ مِنَ الْجَنَّةْ

Allāhumma innī as'aluka khayra 'l-mas'alati wa khayra 'd-du'ā'i wa khayra 'n-najāḥi wa khayra 'l-'ilmi, wa khayra 'l-'amali wa khayra 'th-thawābi wa khayra 'l-ḥayāti wa khayra 'l-mamāti, wa thabbitnī wa thaqqi 'l-mawāzīnī wa ḥaqqiq imānī w 'arfa' darajātī wa taqabbal ṣalātī w 'aghfir lī khatīyāti wa as'aluka 'l-'ulā min al-jannah.

O Allāh! I ask You for the best affair, the best supplication, the best success, the best Knowledge, the best deed, the best reward, the best life, and the best death. Keep me upright, make my scale heavy, confirm my faith, raise high my status, accept my prayer, and forgive my sins. I ask You for high positions in Paradise.

اللَّهُمَّ إِنِّى أَسَأَلُكَ مُوجِبَاتِ رَحْمَتِكَ وَعَزَائِمَ مَغْفِرَتِكَ وَالسَّلَامَةَ مِنْ كُلِّ إِثْمٍ وَالْغَنِيمَةَ مِنْ كُلِّ بِرٍّ وَالْفَوْزَ بِالْجَنَّةِ وَالنَّجَاةَ مِنَ النَّارْ

Allāhumma innī as'aluka mūjibāti raḥmatika wa ʿazā'ima maghfiratik, wa 's-salāmata min kulli ithmin wa 'l-ghanīmata min kulli birrin wa 'l-fawza bi 'l-jannati wa 'n-najāta min an-nār.

O Allāh! I beg You for that which incites Your Mercy and the means of Your Forgiveness, safety from every sin, the benefit from every good deed, success in attaining Paradise and deliverance from the Fire.

اللَّهُمَّ أحْسِنْ عَاقِبَتَنَا فِى الْأُمورِ كُلِّهَا وَأَجِرْنَا مِنْ خِزْيِ الدُّنْيَا وَعَذَابِ الْأَخِرَةْ

Allāhumma 'ḥsin ʿāqibatanā fi 'l-umūri kullihā wa ajirnā min khizyī 'd-dunyā wa ʿadhābi 'l-ākhirah.

O Allāh! I ask You for wellbeing in all our concerns. Save us from the disgrace of life and the torment of the Hereafter.

اللَّهُمَّ أقْسِمْ لَنَا مِنْ خَشْيَتِكَ مَا تَحُولُ بِهِ بَيْنَنَا وَبَيْنَ مَعْصِيَتِكَ وَمِنْ
طَاعَتِكَ مَاتُبَلِّغُنَا بِهَا جَنَّتَكَ وَمِنَ الْيَقِينِ مَا تُهَوِّنُ بِهِ عَلَيْنَا مِنْ
مَصَائِبَ الدُّنْيَا وَمَتِّعْنَا بِأَسْمَاعِنَا وَأَبْصَارِنَا وَقُوَّتِنَا مَاأَحْيَيْتَنَا
وَأجْعَلْهُ الْوَارِثَ مَنَّا وَأجْعَل ثَأْرَنَا عَلَى مَنْ ظَلَمَنَا وَأَنْصُرْنَا عَلَى مَنْ
عَادَانَا وَلَا تَجْعَلْ مُصِيبَتَنَا فِى دِينِنَا وَلَا تَجْعَلِ الدُّنْيَا أَكْبَرَ هَمِّنَا
وَلَا مَبْلَغَ عِلْمِنَا وَلَا تُسَلِّطْ عَلَيْنَا مِنْ لَا يَرْحَمُنَا

Allāhumma 'qsim lanā min khashīyatika mā taḥūlu baynanā wa bayna maʿṣīyatika wa min ṭāʿatika mā tuballighunā bihā jannataka wa min al-yaqīni mā tuhawwinu bihī ʿalaynā min maṣā'iba 'd-dunyā wa mattiʿnā bi asmāʿinā wa abṣārinā wa quwwatinā mā aḥyaytanā w 'ajʿalhu 'l-wāritha minnā w 'ajʿal thā'ranā ʿalā man ẓalamanā wa 'n-ṣurnā ʿalā man ʿādānā wa lā tajʿal muṣībatanā fī dīninā wa lā tajʿalī 'd-dunyā akbara ḥamminā wa lā mablagha ʿilminā wa lā tusalliṭ ʿalaynā man lā yarḥamunā.

O Allāh! Grant us Your Fear and Mercy which may stand between us in acts of disobedience to You; and such obedience as will take us to Your Paradise; and such deep faith that may render all worldly losses as worthless for us. O Allāh! Grant us the favor of utilizing our sense of hearing, sight and physical strength to our advantage and continue this favor even after we are no more. Take our revenge from him who oppresses us. Grant us victory over him who shows enmity toward us. Do not put us on trial concerning religion. Do not make worldly goods the chief objects of our lives. Do not make this world the limit of our knowledge and wisdom, nor entrust us under the charge of a person who shows no mercy to us.

اللَّهُمَّ لَا تَدَعْ لَنَا ذَنْبًا إِلَّا غَفَرْتَهُ وَلَا هَمًّا إِلَّا فَرَّجْتَهُ وَلَا دَيْنًا إِلَّا قَضَيْتَهُ وَلَا حَاجَةً مِنْ حَوَائِجِ الدُّنْيَا وَالْأَخِرَةَ إِلَّا قَضَيْتَهَا يَارَبَّ الْعَالَمِينْ

Allāhumma lā tadaʿ lanā dhanban illā ghafartahu wa lā hamman illā farrajtahu wa lā daynan illā qaḍaytahu wa lā ḥājatan min ḥawā'iji 'd-dunyā wa 'l-ākhirata illā qaḍaytahā yā Rabba 'l-ʿālamīn.

O Allāh! Do not leave for us any sin unless You forgave it, any sadness unless You removed it, any debt unless You settled it, and any single need among the many needs of this life as well as the life to come without fulfilling it, O the Lord of the Worlds!

رَبَّنَا آتِنَا فِى الدُّنْيَا حَسَنَةً وَفِى الْأَخِرَةَ حَسَنَةً وَقِنَا عَذَابَ النَّارْ وَأَدْخِلْنَا الْجَنَّةَ مَعَ الْأَبْرَارِ بِرَحْمَتِكَ يَا عَزِيزُ يَا غَفَّارَ، يَا كَرِيمُ يَا سَتَّارُ، يَا رَبَّ الْعَالَمِينَ رَبِّ اغْفِرْ وَارْحَمْ وَأَنْتَ خَيْرُ الرَّاحِمِينْ.

Rabbanā ātinā fi 'd-dunyā ḥasanatan wa fi 'l-ākhirati ḥasanatan wa qinā ʿadhāba 'n-nār w 'ad-khilna 'l-jannata maʿa 'l-abrār, bi raḥmatika yā ʿAzīzu yā

Ghaffār, yā Karīmu yā Sattār, yā Rabba 'l-ʿālamīn. Rabbi 'ghfir wa 'rḥam wa anta khayru 'r-rāḥimīn.

O Allāh! Give us goodness in this world and goodness in the Hereafter, and protect us from the torment of the Hellfire, and admit us into Paradise along with those who fulfill their vows, by Your Mercy, O Forgiver, O The Most Generous, O the Veiler of Sins, O the Lord of the Worlds! "*(Say, O Muḥammad:) O Allāh! Forgive and have mercy, for You are the best of those who show mercy.*" (23:118)

اللَّهُمَّ ثَبِّتْنَا عَلَى الْإِيمَانْ، اللَّهُمَّ ثَبِّتْنَا عَلَى الْإِسْلَامْ، اللَّهُمَّ ثَبِّتْنَا عَلَى الْإِحْسَانْ.

Allāhumma thabbitnā ʿalā 'l-īmān! Allāhumma thabbitnā ʿalā 'l-Islām! Allāhumma thabbitnā ʿalā 'l-iḥsān.

O Allāh! Make us firm upon faith. O Allāh! Make us firm upon Islam. O Allāh! Make us firm upon sincerity.

اللَّهُمَّ أَجِرنَا مِنْ عَذَابِ الْقَبْرِ وَمِنْ عَذَابِ النَّارِ وَمِنْ فِتْنَةِ الْمَحْيَا وَالْمَمَاتِ وَمِنْ فِتْنَةِ الْمَسِيحِ الدَّجَّالِ.

Allāhumma ajirnā min ʿadhābi 'l-qabri wa min ʿadhābi 'n-nār wa min fitnati 'l-maḥyā wa 'l-mamāti wa min fitnati 'l-masīḥi 'd-dajjāl

O Allāh! We seek refuge with You from the punishment of the grave, from the punishment of the Hellfire, from the tribulations of life and death, and from the tribulation of the False Messiah.

اللَّهُمَّ إِنَّا نَسْأَلُكَ مِنْ خَيْرِ مَا سَأَلَكَ مِنْهُ سَيِّدُنَا وَنَبِيُّنَا مُحَمَّدٌ صَلَّى اللهُ عَلَيْهِ وَسَلَّمَ وَنَسْتَعِيذُكَ مِنْ شَرِّ مَا اسْتَعَاذَكَ مِنْهُ سَيِّدُنَا وَنَبِيُّنَا مُحَمَّدٍ صَلَّى اللهُ عَلَيْهِ وَسَلَّمَ. اللَّهُمَّ كُنْ لَنَا وَلَا تَكُنْ عَلَيْنَا.

Allāhuma innā nas'aluka min khayri mā sa'alaka minhu sayyīdunā wa Nabīyyunā Muḥammadin, ṣalla 'Llāhu ʿalayhi wa sallam, wa nastaʿīdhuka min sharri māstaʿādhaka minhu sayyīdunā wa Nabīyyunā Muḥammadin, ṣalla 'Llāhu ʿalayhi wa sallam. Allāhumma kun lanā wa lā takun ʿalaynā.

O Allāh, we ask You from the best of what our Master and Prophet Muḥammad, peace and blessings be upon him, asked You, and we seek Your refuge from the evil which our Master and Prophet Muḥammad, peace and blessings be upon him, sought refuge in You from. O Allāh! Be for us and don't be against us.

اللَّهُمَّ اشْفِنَا وَأُشْفِ مَرْضَانَا وَمَرْضَى الْمُسْلِمِينَ وَعَافِنَا وَعَافِ مَرَضَانَا وَمَرْضَى الْمُسْلِمِينْ.

Allāhumma 'shfinā w 'ashfi marḍānā wa marḍa 'l-muslimīn, wa ʿafinā wa ʿāfi marḍānā wa marḍa 'l-muslimīn.

O Allāh! Give us cure and give cure to our diseases and the diseases of the Muslims in general. Pardon us and pardon our diseases and the diseases of the Muslims.

وَأَمِدَّ بِعُمْرِى لِإِدْرَاكِ عَصْرِ صَاحِبِ الزَّمَانْ سَيِّدُنَا مُحَمَّدُ الْمَهْدِى عَلَيْهِ السَّلَامْ وَسَيِّدُنَا عِيسَى عَلَيْهِ السَّلَامْ

Wa amidda bi ʿumrī li-idrāki ʿaṣri Ṣāhibi 'z-Zamān Sayyīdinā Muḥammadu 'l-Mahdī ʿalayhi 's-salām wa Sayyīdinā ʿĪsā ʿalayhi 's-salām.

And extend our lives until we reach the time of the owner of time, our Master Muḥammad al-Mahdī, peace be upon him, and Sayyīdinā ʿĪsā, peace be upon him.

اللَّهُمَّ إِنَّا نَتَوَسَّلُ إِلَيْكَ بِنَبِيِّكَ الْمُصْطَفَى سَيِّدِنَا مُحَمَّدْ صَلَّى اللهُ عَلَيْهِ وَسَلَّمْ. يَا مُحَمَّدْ ! إِنَّا نَتَوَجَّهُ بِكَ إِلَى رَبِّنَا فَاشْفَعْ لَنَا عِنْدَ الْمَوْلَى الْعَظِيمَ، يَا نِعْمَ الرَّسُولُ الطَّاهِرُ.اللَّهُمَّ شَفِّعْهُ فِينَا بِجَاهِهِ عِنْدَكَ يَا الله.

Allāhumma innā natawassalu ilayka bi nabīyyika 'l-Musṭafā, Sayyīdinā Muḥammad, ṣalla 'Llāhu ʿalayhi wa sallam. Yā Muḥammad! Innā natawajjahu bika ilā rabbinā fashfaʿ lanā ʿinda 'l-mawla 'l-aẓīm, yā niʿma 'r-Rasūlu 'ṭ-Ṭāhir. Allāhumma shaffiʿhu fīnā bi jāhihi ʿindaka, yā Allāh.

O Allāh, we intercede to You through Your Prophet, the Chosen One, our Master Muḥammad, peace and blessings be upon him. O Muḥammad, we direct ourselves through you to our Lord, so intercede for us with our master, O Purest Prophet. O Allāh! Accept his intercession for us according to his status with You.

أهدآ

Ihdā

Dedication

بِسْمِ اللهِ الرَّحْمٰنِ الرَّحِيمِ نَهْدِى ثَوَابَ مَا قَرَأْنَا خَتْمُ الْقُرْآنْ إِلَى حَضْرَةِ النَّبِيِّ صَلَّى اللهُ عَلَيْهِ وَسَلَّمْ وآلِهِ وَصَحْبِهِ الْكِرَامْ وَإِلَى أَرْوَاحِ إِخْوَانِهِ مِنَ الْأَنْبِيَاءِ وَالْمُرْسَلِينَ وَ خُدَمَاءِ شَرَائِعِهِم وَإِلَى أَرْوَاحِ الْأَئِمَّةِ الْأَرْبَعَةْ وَإِلَى أَرْوَاحِ مشَائِخِنَا فِى الطَّرِيقَةِ النَّقْشبَنْدِيَّةِ الْعَلِيَّةْ خَاصَّةً إِلَى رُوحِ إِمَامِ الطَّرِيقَةُ وَغَوْثُ الْخَلِيقَة خَوَاجه بَهَاءِ الدِّينِ نَقْشبَنْدِ مُحَمَّدَ الأُوَيْسِيُّ الْبُخَارِى، وَإِلَى سُلْطَانُ الْأَوْلِيَاءِ الشَّيْخْ عَبْدُ اللهِ الفَائِزِ الدَّاغِسْتَانِىْ وَإِلَى شَيْخُنَا مُحَمَّدَ نَاظِمَ الْحَقَّانِى مُؤَيِّدَ الدِّينِ وَسَائِرِ سَادَاتِنَا وَالصِدِّيقِينَا

Bismillāhi 'r-Raḥmāni 'r-Raḥīm. Nahdī thāwāba mā qarā'nā khatmu 'l-qurān ilā ḥadratin Nabīyyi ṣalla 'Llāhu ʿalayhi wa sallama wa ālihi wa ṣaḥbihi 'l-kirām wa ilā arwāḥi ikhwānihi min al-anbīyā'i wa 'l-mursalīn wa khudamā'i sharāʿihim wa ilā arwāḥi 'l-a'immati 'l-arbaʿa wa ilā arwāḥi mashāykhinā fi 'ṭ-ṭarīqati-n-Naqshbandīyyati-l-ʿalīyya, khāṣṣatan ilā rūḥi īmāmi 'ṭ-

ṭarīqati wa ghawthi 'l-khalīqati Khwājā Bahā'uddīn Naqshband Muḥammad al-Uwaysī al-Bukhārī, wa ilā Sulṭānu 'l-Awlīyā Shaykh 'AbdAllāh al-Fā'iz ad-Dāghestānī wa ilā Shaykhinā Muḥammad Nāẓim al-Ḥaqqānī Mu'ayyad ad-dīn wa sā'iri sādātinā wa 'ṣ-ṣiddiqīnā.

O Allāh! Grant that the merit of what we have read, and the light of what we have recited, are considered an offering and gift from us to the soul of our Prophet Muḥammad ﷺ, and to the souls of the prophets and saints, in particular, the soul of the Imam of the *Ṭarīqah* and arch-Intercessor of the created world, Khāwajā Bahāuddīn an-Naqshband Muḥammad al-Uwaysī 'l-Bukhārī, and our venerable teacher and master, the Sulṭān of Saints, our Shaykh 'AbdAllāh Dāghestānī, and our master Shaykh Nāẓim al-Ḥaqqānī, Supporter of the Faith, and to all our masters and to the righteous.

وَإِلَى أَرْوَاحِ آبَائِنَا وَأُمَّهَاتِنَا وأَجْدَادِنا وَجَدَّاتِنَا وأَبْنَائِنَا وَبَنَاتِنَا
وَإِخْوَانِنَا وَأَخَوَاتِنَا وَأَعْمَامِنَا وَعَمَّاتِنَا وَأَخْوَالِنَا وَخَالَاتِنَا وَإِلَى أَهْلِ
الْعَبَا وَأَهْلِ بَيْتِنَا وَإِلَى الْمَظْلُومِينَ السَّادَاتِ وَالشُّرَفَاءِ وَالْغُزَاةِ
وَالْحُجَّاجِ وَالْمُعْتَمِرِينَ فِى بَرِّكَ وَبَحْرِكَ وَجَوِّكَ مِنْ أُمَّةِ مُحَمَّدٍ عَامَّةً
أَجْمَعِينَ وَإِلَى أَرْوَاحِ أَهْلِ بَيْتِ حَبِيبِكَ الْمُصْطَفَى سَيِّدِنَا مُحَمَّدٍ
صَلَّى اللَّهُ عَلَيْهِ وَسَلَّمَ وَأَهْلِ بَيْتِنَا خَاصَّةً إِلَى آبَائِى وَأَجْدَادِى...

Wa ilā arwāḥi ābā'inā wa ummahātina wa ajdādinā wa jaddātinā wa abnā'inā wa banātinā wa ikhwāninā wa akhawātinā wa ʿamāminā wa ʿamātinā wa akhwālinā wa khālātinā wa ilā āhli 'l-ʿabā wa āhli baytinā wa ila 'l-maẓlūmīna 's-sādāti wa 'sh-shurafā'i wa 'l-ghuzāti wa 'l-ḥujjāji wa 'l-muʿtamirīna fī barrika wa baḥrika wa jawwika min ummati Muḥammadin ʿammatin ajmaʿīn wa ilā arwāḥi āhli bayti Ḥabībika 'l-Musṭafā Sayyidinā Muḥammad ṣalla 'Llāhu ʿalayhi wa sallama wa āhli baytinā.

And to the souls of our fathers, mothers, grandfathers, grandmothers, sons and daughters, brothers and sisters, uncles and aunts, and to the people of the Prophetic Mantle, our household, and to the oppressed from among the descendants of the Prophet, peace be upon him, soldiers, pilgrims in your land, sea and air from the community of Muḥammad ﷺ generally, and to the souls of the household of Your Beloved Chosen One, our Master Muḥammad, peace be upon him, and to our household.

يَا رَبَّنَا تَقَبَّلْ مِنَّا وَلِجَمِيعِ الْمُؤْمِنِينَ وَالْمُؤْمِنَاتِ وَالْمُسْلِمِينَ الْمُسْلِمَاتِ الْأَحْيَاءِ مِنْهُمْ وَالْأَمْوَاتِ إِنَّكَ غُفُورٌ رَحِيمٌ يَا رَبَّ الْعَالَمِينَ وَصَلَّى اللهُ عَلَى سَيِّدِنَا وَنَبِيِّنَا مُحَمَّدٍ وَعَلَى آلِهِ وَصَحْبِهِ أَجْمَعِينَ سُبْحَانَ رَبِّكَ رَبِّ الْعِزَّةِ عَمَّا يَصِفُونَ وَسَلَامٌ عَلَى الْمُرْسَلِينَ وَالْحَمْدُ لِلَّهِ رَبِّ الْعَالَمِينَ الْفَاتِحَةُ

Yā Rabbanā, taqabbal minnā wa li jamiʿī 'l-mu'minīna wa 'l-mu'mināt wa 'l-muslimīna wa 'l-muslimāti 'l-aḥyā'i minhum wa 'l-amwāt, innaka Ghafūru 'r-Raḥīmun yā Rabba 'l-ʿālamīn.

Wa ṣalla 'Llāhu ʿalā Sayyīdīnā wa Nabīyyīnā Muḥammadin wa ʿalā ālihi wa ṣaḥbihi ajmaʿīn. Subḥāna Rabbika Rabbi 'l-ʿizzati ʿammā yaṣifūn wa salāmun ʿalā 'l-mursalīn wa 'l-ḥamdulillāh Rabbi 'l-ʿālamīn. Al-Fātiḥa!

Our Lord! Accept from us and from all Believing men and women and from all Muslim men and women, those living and deceased. Indeed, You are the Most Forgiving, the Most Merciful, the Lord of All the Worlds. May Allāh send His Benedictions upon our Master and Prophet, Muḥammad ﷺ, his Family and all his Companions. May Our Lord, the Lord of Majesty, be exalted above all descriptions, and peace be upon the Messengers, and all praise for Allāh, the Lord of the Worlds.

Al-Fātiḥa.